Risk Analysis

Risk Analysis

Second Edition

Terje Aven

University of Stavanger, Norway

This edition first published 2015
© 2015 John Wiley & Sons, Ltd

Registered office
John Wiley & Sons Ltd, The Atrium, Southern Gate, Chichester, West Sussex, PO19 8SQ, United Kingdom

For details of our global editorial offices, for customer services and for information about how to apply for permission to reuse the copyright material in this book please see our website at www.wiley.com.

Library of Congress Cataloging-in-Publication Data

Aven, Terje.
    Risk analysis / Terje Aven. – Second edition.
        pages cm
    Previous edition: 2008.
    Includes bibliographical references and index.
    ISBN 978-1-119-05779-6 (cloth)
  1.   Risk assessment–Mathematical models.   2.   Risk–Mathematical models.
3.   Uncertainty–Mathematical models.   I. Title.
    HD61.A938 2015
    338.5–dc23

                                                    2015018045

A catalogue record for this book is available from the British Library.

ISBN: 9781119057796

Set in 10/12pt, Times by SPi Global, Chennai, India.
Printed and bound in Singapore by Markono Print Media Pte Ltd

1   2015

Contents

Preface

This book is about risk analysis – basic ideas, principles and methods. Both theory and practice are covered. A number of books exist presenting the many risk analysis methods and tools, such as fault tree analysis, event tree analysis and Bayesian networks. In this book we go one step back and discuss the role of the analyses in risk management. How such analyses should be planned, executed and used, such that they meet the professional standards for risk analyses and at the same time are useful in a practical decision-making context. In the book we review the common risk analysis methods, but the emphasis is placed on the context and applications. By using examples from different areas, we highlight the various elements that are part of the planning, execution and use of the risk analysis method. What are the main challenges we face? What type of methods should we choose? How can we avoid scientific mistakes? The examples used are taken from, among others, the transport sector, the petroleum industry and ICT (Information and Communication Technology). For each example we define a decision-making problem, and show how the analyses can be used to provide adequate decision support. The book covers both safety (accidental events) and security (intentional acts).

This book is based on the recommended approach to risk analysis described and discussed in Aven (2012a,d). The basic idea is that risk analysis should produce a broad risk picture, highlighting uncertainties beyond expected values and probabilities. The aim of the risk analysis is to predict unknown physical quantities, such as the explosion pressure, the number of fatalities, costs and so on, and assess uncertainties. A probability is not a perfect tool for expressing the uncertainties we have to acknowledge that the assigned probabilities are subjective probabilities conditional on a specific background knowledge. The assigned probabilities could produce poor predictions. The main component of risk is uncertainty, not probability. Surprises relative to the assigned probabilities may occur and by just addressing probabilities such surprises may be overlooked.

It has been a goal to provide a simplified presentation of the material, without diminishing the requirement for precision and accuracy. In this book, technicalities are reduced to a minimum, instead ideas and principles are highlighted. Reading the book requires no special background, but for certain parts it would be beneficial to have a knowledge of basic probability theory and statistics. It has, however, been a goal to reduce the dependency on extensive prior knowledge of probability theory and statistics. The key statistical concepts are introduced and discussed thoroughly in the book. Appendix A summarises some basic probability theory and statistical analysis. This makes the book more self-contained, and it gives the book the required sharpness with respect to relevant concepts and tools.

We have also included a brief appendix covering basic reliability analysis, so that the reader can obtain the necessary background for calculating the reliability of a safety system.

This book is primarily about planning, execution and use of risk analyses, and it provides clear recommendations and guidance in this context. However, it is not a recipe-book, telling you which risk analysis methods should be used in different situations. What is covered, is the general thinking process related to the planning, execution and use of risk analyses. Examples are provided to illustrate this process.

This book is based on and relates to the research literature in the field of risk, risk analysis and risk management.

Some of the premises for the approach taken in the book as well as some areas of scientific dispute are looked into in a special 'Discussion' chapter (Chapter 13). The issues addressed include the risk concept, the use of risk acceptance criteria and the definition of safety critical systems.

The target audience for the book is primarily professionals within the risk analysis and risk management fields, but others, in particular managers and decision-makers, can also benefit from the book. All those working with risk-related problems need to understand the fundamental principles of risk analysis.

This book is based on a Norwegian book on risk analysis (Aven et al. 2008), with co-authors Willy Røed and Hermann S. Wiencke. The present version is, however, more advanced and includes topics that are not included in Aven et al. (2008).

The terminology used in the book is summarised in Appendix D.

Our approach means a humble attitude to risk and the possession of the truth, and hopefully it will be more attractive also to social scientists and others, who have strongly criticised the prevalent thinking of risk analysis and evaluation in the engineering environment. Our way of thinking, to a large extent, integrates technical and economic risk analyses and the social scientist perspectives on risk. As a main component of risk is uncertainty about the world, risk perception has a role to play to guide decision-makers. Professional risk analysts do not have the exclusive right to describe risk.

Acknowledgements

A number of individuals have provided helpful comments and suggestions to this book. In particular, I would like to acknowledge my co-authors of Aven et al. (2008), Willy Røed and Hermann S. Wiencke. Chapters 7 and 11 are mainly due to Willy and

Hermann; thanks to both. I am also grateful to Eirik B. Abrahamsen and Roger Flage for the great deal of time and effort they spent reading and preparing comments.

For financial support, thanks to the University of Stavanger, and the Research Council of Norway.

I also acknowledge the editing and production staff at Wiley for their careful work.

January 2009, Terje Aven

Preface Second Edition

In this second edition I have updated the book with the most recent developments related to risk conceptualization and related issues on risk assessments and their use. Chapter 2 is to large extent rewritten, and some adjustments have also been made in the other chapters to be in line with the new Chapter 2. In the discussion Chapter 13, a new section on the difference between risk as seen from the perspectives of the analysts and management, is included. Also a number of misprints have been corrected.

Terje Aven

1

What is a risk analysis?

A main objective of a risk analysis is to describe risk, that is, to present an informative risk picture. Figure 1.1 illustrates important building blocks of such a risk picture. Located at the centre of the figure is the initiating event (the hazard, the threat, the opportunity), which we denote by A. In the example, the event is that a person (John) contracts a specific disease. An important task in the risk analysis is to identify such initiating events. In our example, we may be concerned about various diseases that could affect the person. The left side of the figure illustrates the causal picture that may lead to the event A. The right side describes the possible consequences of A.

On the left side are barriers that are introduced to prevent the event A from occurring; these are the probability reducing or preventive barriers. Examples of such barriers are medical check-ups/examinations, vaccinations and limiting the exposure to contamination sources. On the right side are barriers to prevent the disease (event A) from bringing about serious consequences, the consequence-reducing barriers. Examples of such barriers are medication and surgery. The occurrence of A and performance of the various barriers are influenced by a number of factors – the so-called risk-influencing or performance-influencing factors. Examples are the quality of the medical check-ups; the effectiveness of the vaccine, drug or surgery; what is known about the disease and what causes it; lifestyle, nutrition and inheritance and genes.

Figure 1.1 is often referred to as a *bow-tie* diagram. We will refer to it many times later in the book when the risk picture is being discussed.

We refer to the event A as an initiating event. When the consequences are obviously negative, the term 'undesirable event' is used. We also use terms such as hazards and threats. We say there is a fire hazard or that we are faced with a terrorist threat. We can also use the term initiating event in connection with an opportunity. An example is the opportunity that arises if a competitor goes bankrupt or his reputation is damaged.

Risk Analysis, Second Edition. Terje Aven.
© 2015 John Wiley & Sons, Ltd. Published 2015 by John Wiley & Sons, Ltd.

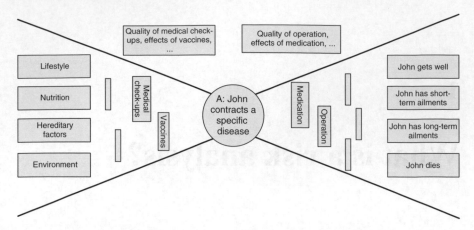

Figure 1.1   Example of a bow-tie.

Table 1.1   Main categories of risk analysis methods.

Main category	Type of analysis	Description
Simplified risk analysis	Qualitative	Simplified risk analysis is an informal procedure that establishes the risk picture using brainstorming sessions and group discussions. The risk might be presented on a coarse scale, for example, low, moderate or high, making no use of formalised risk analysis methods.
Standard risk analysis	Qualitative or quantitative	Standard risk analysis is a more formalised procedure in which recognised risk analysis methods are used, such as Hazard and Operability study (HAZOP) and coarse risk analysis, to name a few. Risk matrices are often used to present the results.
Model-based risk analysis	Primarily quantitative	Model-based risk analysis makes use of techniques such as event tree analysis and fault tree analysis to calculate risk.

The risk analysis shall identify the relevant initiating events and develop the causal and consequence picture. How this is done depends on which method is used and how the results are to be used. However, the intent is always the same: to describe risk.

In this book, we differentiate between three main categories of risk analysis methods: simplified risk analysis, standard risk analysis and model-based risk analysis. These three categories of methods are described in more detail in Table 1.1.

The different methods mentioned in the table will be discussed in Chapter 6.

Reflection

An overview of historical data (e.g. accident events) is established. Does this constitute a risk analysis?

No, not in isolation. Such data describe what happened, and the numbers say something about the past. Only when we address the future (e.g. the number of fatalities in the coming year) does the risk concept apply. To analyse what will happen, we can decide to make use of the historical numbers, and the statistics will then provide an expression for risk. In this way, we are conducting a risk analysis.

1.1   Why risk analysis?

By carrying out a risk analysis one can

- establish a risk picture;

- compare different alternatives and solutions in terms of risk;

- identify factors, conditions, activities, systems, components and so on that are important (critical) with respect to risk; and

- demonstrate the effect of various measures on risk.

This provides a basis for the following:

- Choosing between various alternative solutions and activities while in the planning phase of a system.

- Choosing between alternative designs of a solution or a measure. What measures can be implemented to make the system less vulnerable in the sense that it can better tolerate loads and stresses?

- Drawing conclusions on whether various solutions and measures meet the stated requirements.

- Setting requirements for various solutions and measures, for example, related to the performance of the preparedness systems.

- Documenting an acceptable safety and risk level.

Risk analyses can be carried out at various phases in the life time of a system, that is, from the early concept phase, through the more detailed planning phases and the construction phase, up to the operation and decommissioning phases.

Risk analyses are often performed to satisfy regulatory requirements. It is, of course, important to satisfy these requirements, but the driving force for carrying out a risk analysis should not be this alone, if one wishes to fully utilise the potential of the analysis. The main reason for conducting a risk analysis is to support decision-making. The analysis can provide an important basis for finding the right balance between different concerns, such as safety and costs.

We need to distinguish between the planning phase and the operational phase. When we design a system, we often have considerable flexibility and can choose among many different solutions, while often having limited access to detailed information on these solutions. The risk analysis in such cases provides a basis for comparing the various alternatives. The fact that we have many possible decision alternatives and limited detailed information implies, as a rule, that one will have to use a relatively coarse analysis method. As one gradually gains more knowledge regarding the final solution, more detailed analysis methods will become possible. All along, one must balance the demand for precision with the demand for decision support. There is no point in carrying out detailed analyses if the results arrive too late to affect the decisions.

In the operating phase, we often have access to experience data, for example, historical data, on the number of equipment and systems failures. In such cases, one can choose a more detailed analysis method and study these systems specifically. However, here the decision alternatives are often limited. It is easier by far to make changes 'on paper' in planning phases than to make changes to existing systems in the operating phase. Risk analyses have, therefore, had their greatest application in the planning phases. In this book, however, we do not limit ourselves to these phases. Risk analyses are useful in all phases, but the methods applied must be suited to the need.

1.2   Risk management

Risk management is defined as all measures and activities carried out to manage risk. Risk management deals with balancing the conflicts inherent in exploring opportunities on the one hand and avoiding losses, accidents and disasters on the other (Aven and Vinnem 2007).

Risk management relates to all activities, conditions and events that can affect the organisation and its ability to reach the organisation's goals and vision. To be more specific, we will consider an enterprise, for example, a company. Identification of which activities, conditions and events are important will depend on the enterprise and its goals and vision.

In many enterprises, the risk management is divided into three main categories: strategic risk, financial risk and operational risk.

Strategic risk is risk where the consequences for the enterprise are influenced by mergers and acquisitions, technology, competition, political conditions, laws and regulations, labour market and so on.

Financial risk is risk where the consequences for the enterprise are influenced by the market (associated with changes in the value of an investment due to movements in market factors: the stock prices, interest rates, foreign exchange rates and commodity prices), credit issues (associated with a debtor's failure to meet its obligations in accordance with agreed terms) and liquidity issues, reflecting lack of access to cash; the difficulty of selling an asset in a timely manner, that is, quickly enough to prevent a loss (or make the required profit).

Operational risk is risk where the consequences for the enterprise are a result of safety- or security-related issues (accidental events, intentional acts, etc.).

For an enterprise to become successful in its implementation of risk management, the top management needs to be involved, and activities must be put into effect on many levels. Some important points to ensure success are:

- Establishment of a strategy for risk management, that is, the principles of how the enterprise defines and runs the risk management. Should one simply follow the regulatory requirements (minimal requirements) or should one be the 'best in the class'? We refer to Section 1.3.

- Establishment of a risk management process for the enterprise, that is, formal processes and routines that the enterprise has to follow.

- Establishment of management structures, with roles and responsibilities, such that the risk analysis process becomes integrated into the organisation.

- Implementation of analyses and support systems, for example, risk analysis tools and recording systems for occurrences of various types of events.

- Communication, training and development of a risk management culture, so that the competence, understanding and motivation level within the organisation is enhanced.

The risk analysis process is a central part of the risk management, and has a basic structure that is independent of its area of application. There are several ways of presenting the risk analysis process, but most structures contain the following three key elements:

- Planning

- Risk assessment (execution)

- Risk treatment (use).

In this book, we use the term 'risk analysis process', when we talk about the three main phases: planning, risk assessment and risk treatment, while we use 'risk management process' when we include other management elements also, which are not directly linked to the risk analysis.

We make a clear distinction between the terms risk analysis, risk evaluation and risk assessment:

$$\text{Risk analysis} + \text{Risk evaluation} = \text{Risk assessment}$$

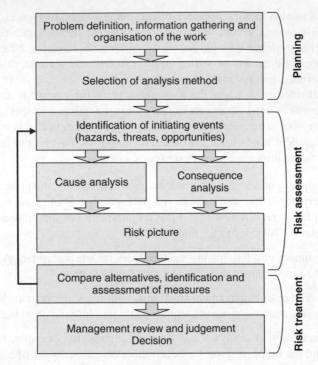

Figure 1.2   The main steps of the risk analysis process.

The results from the risk analysis are evaluated. How does alternative I compare with alternative II? Is the risk too high? Is there a need to implement risk-reducing measures? We use the term risk assessment to mean both the analysis and the evaluation.

Risk assessment is followed by risk treatment. This represents the process and implementation of measures to modify risk, including tools to avoid, reduce, optimise, transfer and retain risk. Transfer of risk means to share with another party the benefits or potential losses connected with a risk. Insurance is a common type of risk transfer.

Figure 1.2 shows the main steps of the risk analysis process. We will frequently refer to this figure in the forthcoming chapters. It forms the basis for the structure of and discussions in Chapters 3, 4 and 5.

1.2.1   Decision-making under uncertainty

Risk management often involves decision-making in situations characterised by high risk and large uncertainties, and such decision-making presents a challenge in that it is difficult to predict the consequences (outcomes) of the decisions. Generally, the decision process includes the following elements:

1. The decision situation and the stakeholders (interested parties):
   – What is the decision to be made?
   – What are the alternatives?
   – What are the boundary conditions?
   – Who is affected by the decision?
   – Who will make the decision?
   – What strategies are to be used to reach a decision?

2. Goal-setting, preferences and performance measures:
   – What do the various interested parties want?
   – How to weigh the pros and cons?
   – How to express the performance of the various alternatives?

3. The use of various means, including various forms of analyses to support the decision-making:
   – Risk analyses
   – Cost-benefit analyses (see Chapter 3)
   – Cost-effectiveness analyses (see Chapter 3).

4. Review and judgement by the decision-maker. Decision.

A model for decision-making, based on the above elements, is presented in Figure 1.3. The starting point is a decision problem, and often this is stated as a problem of choosing between a set of alternatives, all meeting some stated goals and requirements. In the early phase of the process, many alternatives that are more or less precisely defined are considered. Various forms of analyses provide

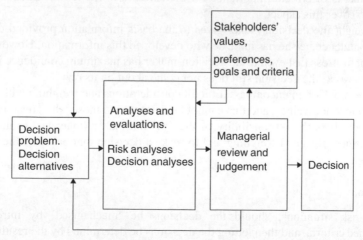

Figure 1.3   A model for decision-making under uncertainty (Aven 2012d).

a basis for sorting these and choosing which ones are to be processed further. Finally, the decision-maker must perform a review and judgement of the various alternatives, taking into account the constraints and limitations of the analyses. Then, the decision-maker makes a decision.

This is a simple model of the decision-making process. The model outlines how the process should be implemented. If the model is followed, the process can be documented and traced. The model is, however, not very detailed and specific.

The decision support produced by the analyses must be reviewed by the decision-maker prior to making the decision: What is the background information of the analyses? What are the assumptions and suppositions made? The results from the analyses must be evaluated in the light of factors, such as the following:

- Which decision-making alternatives have been analysed?

- Which performance measures have been assessed?

- The fact that the analyses represent judgements (expert judgements).

- Difficulties in determining the advantages and disadvantages of the different alternatives.

- The fact that the results of the analyses are based on models that are simplifications of the real world and real-world phenomena.

The decision-making basis will seldom be in a format that provides all the answers that are important to the decision-maker. There will always be limitations in the basis information, and the review and judgement described here means that one views the basis in a larger context. Perhaps the analysis did not take into consideration what the various measures mean for the reputation of the enterprise, but this is obviously a factor that is of critical importance for the enterprise. The review and judgement must also cover this aspect.

The weight the decision-maker gives to the basis information provided depends on the confidence he/she has in those who developed this information. However, it is important to stress that even if the decision-maker has maximum confidence in those doing this work, the decision still does not come about on its own.

The decisions often encompass difficult considerations and weighing with respect to uncertainty and values, and this cannot be delegated to those who create the basis information. It is the responsibility of the decision-maker (manager) to undertake such considerations and weighing and to make a decision that balances the various concerns.

Reflection

In high-risk situations, should the decisions be 'mechanised' by introducing pre-defined criteria, and then letting the decisions be determined by the results of the analyses?

No, we need a management review and judgement that places the analyses into a wider context.

Various decision-making strategies can form the basis for the decision. By 'decision-making strategy', we mean the underlying thinking and the principles that are to be followed when making the decision and how the process prior to the decision should be. Of importance to this are the questions of who will be involved and what types of analysis to use.

A decision-making strategy takes into consideration the effect on risk (as it appears in the risk analysis) and the uncertainty dimensions that cannot be captured by the analysis. The result is thus decisions founded both in calculated risk and applications of the *cautionary principle* and *precautionary principle*. The cautionary principle means that caution, for example, by not starting an activity or by implementing measures to reduce risks and uncertainties, shall be the overriding principle when there is uncertainty linked to the consequences, that is, when risk is present (HSE 2001, Aven and Vinnem 2007). The level of caution adopted will, of course, have to be balanced against other concerns, such as costs. However, all industries would introduce some minimum requirements to protect people and the environment, and these requirements can be considered justified by reference to the cautionary principle.

For example, in the Norwegian petroleum industry, it is a regulatory requirement that the living quarters on an installation plant should be protected by fireproof panels of a certain quality, for walls facing process and drilling areas. This is a standard adopted to obtain a minimum safety level. It is based on the established practice of many years of operation in process plants. A fire may occur, which represents a hazard for the personnel, and in the case of such an event, the personnel in the living quarters should be protected. The assigned probability for the living quarters on a specific installation plant being exposed to fire may be judged as low, but we know that fires occur from time to time on such installations. It does not matter whether we calculate a fire probability of x or y, as long as we consider the risks to be significant; and this type of risk has been judged to be significant by the authorities. The justification is experience from similar plants and sound judgements. A fire may occur, since it is not an unlikely event, and we should then be prepared. We need no references to cost–benefit analysis. The requirement is based on cautionary thinking.

Risk analyses, cost–benefit analyses and similar types of analyses are tools providing insights into risks and the trade-offs involved. But they are just tools – with strong limitations. Their results are conditioned on a number of assumptions and suppositions. The analyses do not express objective results. Being cautious also means reflecting this fact. We should not put more emphasis on the predictions and assessments of the analyses than what can be justified by the methods being used.

In the face of uncertainties related to the possible occurrences of hazardous situations and accidents, we are cautious and adopt principles of safety management, such as

- robust design solutions, such that deviations from normal conditions are not leading to hazardous situations and accidents;
- design for flexibility, meaning that it is possible to utilise a new situation and adapt to changes in the frame conditions;

- implementation of safety barriers to reduce the negative consequences of hazardous situations if they should occur, for example, a fire;

- improvement of the performance of barriers by using redundancy, maintenance/testing and so on;

- quality control/quality assurance;

- the precautionary principle, which basically says that in the case of lack of scientific certainty on the possible consequences of an activity, we should implement precautionary measures or not carry out the activity

- the ALARP principle, which says that the risk should be reduced to a level that is As Low As Reasonably Practicable.

Thus, the precautionary principle may be considered a special case of the cautionary principle, as it is applicable in cases of scientific uncertainties (Sandin 1999, Löfstedt 2003, Aven 2011f). There are, however, many definitions of the precautionary principle. The well-known 1992 Rio Declaration uses the following definition:

> In order to protect the environment, the precautionary approach shall be widely applied by States according to their capabilities. Where there are threats of serious or irreversible damage, lack of full scientific certainty shall not be used as a reason for postponing cost-effective measures to prevent environmental degradation.

Seeing beyond environmental protection, a definition such as the following reflects what is a typical way of understanding this principle:

> The precautionary principle expresses that if the consequences of an activity could be serious and subject to scientific uncertainties, then precautionary measures should be taken or the activity should not be carried out.

We refer to Aven (2011f) for further discussion of these principles.

It is prudent to distinguish between management strategies for handling the risk agent (such as a chemical or a technology) from those needed for the risk absorbing system (such as a building, an organism or an ecosystem) (Renn 2005); see also Aven and Renn (2009b). With respect to risk-absorbing systems, robustness and resilience are two main categories of strategies/principles. *Robustness* refers to the insensitivity of performance to deviations from normal conditions. Measures to improve robustness include inserting conservatisms or safety factors as an assurance against individual variation, introducing redundant and diverse safety devices to improve structures against multiple stress situations, reducing the susceptibility of the target organism (e.g. iodine tablets for radiation protection), establishing building codes and zoning laws to protect against natural hazards and improving the organisational capability to initiate, enforce, monitor and revise management actions (high reliability, learning organisations).

A resilient system can withstand or even tolerate surprises. In contrast to robustness, where potential threats are known in advance and the absorbing system needs to be prepared to face these threats, resilience is a protective strategy against unknown or highly uncertain events. Instruments for resilience include strengthening of the immune system, diversification of the means for approaching identical or similar ends, reduction of the overall catastrophic potential or vulnerability even in the absence of a concrete threat, design of systems with flexible response options and improvement of conditions for emergency management and system adaptation. Robustness and resilience are closely linked, but they are not identical and require partially different types of actions and instruments.

The decision-making strategy is dependent on the decision-making situation. The differences are large, from routine operations where codes and standards are used to a large extent, to situations with high risks, where there is a need for comprehensive information about risk.

1.3   Examples: decision situations

In this book, we will present a number of examples of the use of risk analysis. A brief introduction to some of these examples is provided below.

1.3.1   Risk analysis for a tunnel

A road tunnel is under construction. This is a 2-km-long, dual carriageway tunnel, with relatively high traffic volumes. Fire-related ventilation in the tunnel has been dimensioned based on regulatory requirements stating that the project must be able to handle a 20 MW fire, that is, a fire in several vehicles, trucks, and the like. Partway in the construction process, however, new regulatory requirements came into effect stating that the design should withstand a fire of 100 MW, which means a fire involving a heavy goods vehicle or a fire in a hazardous goods transport. To upgrade the fire-related ventilation now, when the tunnel is more or less completed, will lead to significant costs and will delay the opening of the tunnel by 6–12 months.

A risk analysis is carried out to assess the effect of upgrading the ventilation system in accordance with the new regulatory requirements and to assess the effect of alternative safety measures. In the regulations, there is an acceptance for introducing alternative measures if it can be documented that they would lead to an equivalent or higher level of safety. The aim of the risk analysis is to provide a basis for determining which measure or measures should be implemented. The reader is referred to Chapter 7.

1.3.2   Risk analysis for an offshore installation

A significant modification of an offshore installation is to be carried out. This would require more production equipment and result in increased accident risk. An increase in production equipment provides more sources of hydrocarbon leakages that can cause fire and explosion if ignited. The problem is to what extent one should install extra fire protection to reduce the consequences in the event of a fire. A risk analysis is to be carried out to provide a basis for making the decision.

How is this analysis to be carried out? How should the risk be expressed? To what degree should we quantify the risk? We have many years of experience records from the operation of this installation. How can we utilise this information? To what degree is the use of cost–benefit analysis relevant in this context?

The reader is referred to Chapter 8 where these problems are discussed.

1.3.3   Risk analysis related to a cash depot

In May 2005, the NOKAS cash depot moved into its new premises at Gausel close to Stavanger in Norway. NOKAS is owned by Norges Bank (the Central Bank of Norway), DNB (the Norwegian Bank) and others. The area where the building is located is called *Frøystad* and is zoned for industry. The closest neighbour, however, is a cooperative kindergarten, and the NOKAS facility is located not far from a residential area. In light of the risk exposure to the children in the kindergarten and other neighbours – caused by possible robberies – the residents feel that the NOKAS facility must be moved, as the risk is unacceptable. The municipality of Stavanger carried out a process to help them take a position to this question and hired consultants to describe and assess the risk. There was a significant amount of discussion on how the risk management process should be carried out. Here, we deal especially with the risk analysis and how it was used. The central problems to be addressed were:

- How should the risk be expressed?
- Should criteria for acceptable risk level be defined, so that we can compare the results from the risk analysis with these?
- How should one take into consideration the significant uncertainty associated with the future regarding the scope of robberies and which methods the perpetrators will use?
- How are the results of the risk analysis to be communicated?
- How can the results from the analysis be utilised in the municipal administrative process?

The process carried out showed that without a clear understanding of the fundamental risk analysis principles, it is not possible to carry out any meaningful analysis and management of the risk. The reader is referred to the discussion of this example in Chapter 10.

2

What is risk?

A main objective of a risk analysis is to describe risk. To understand what it means, we must know what risk is and how it is expressed. In this chapter, we define what we mean by risk in this book. We also look closer at the concept of vulnerability.

2.1 The risk concept and its description

We consider an activity, real or thought-constructed, for a specified period of time. The activity leads to some future consequences C and these are not known – they are uncertain (U). These two components, C and U, constitute risk:

> The risk concept (C, U) covers (i) that the activity leads to some consequences C, and (ii) that these consequences are not known (U).

The consequences are with respect to something that humans value (health, the environment, assets, etc.). The consequences are often seen in relation to some reference values (planned values, objectives, etc.), and the focus is normally on negative, undesirable consequences. This definition does not, however, distinguish between positive and negative consequences (desirable and undesirable consequences), the point being that the activity results in some consequences (whatever they are). One possible restriction of this definition is introduced by requiring that there exists at least one outcome of C judged as undesirable.

Often we split the consequences into events A (for example, a disease, a gas leakage, a terrorist attack) and their consequences C. Risk is then for short written (A, C, U). The definitions (C, U) and (A, C, U) are equivalent. The shorter notation (C, U) does not represent any loss of generality as C in (C, U) expresses all the consequences of the activity including the events A.

Risk Analysis, Second Edition. Terje Aven.
© 2015 John Wiley & Sons, Ltd. Published 2015 by John Wiley & Sons, Ltd.

As an illustration of the risk concept, think of a person's life where our focus is on his/her health condition. Now he/she is 40 years old. We are concerned about the health risk for this person for a specific period of time or the rest of his/her life. The consequences in this case relate to the occurrence or non-occurrence of specific diseases (known or unknown types) and other plagues, their time of occurrence and their consequences for the person (he/she may die, suffer, etc.). Following this definition, risk exists objectively in the sense of intersubjectivity. No one (with normal senses) would dispute that a human being can get some diseases and that we do not know in advance whether these diseases will occur or not. This definition of risk is general and also includes surprising events, for example, the person can get a new type of disease.

Thus, the risk concept has been defined. However, this concept does not give us a tool for assessing and managing risk. For this purpose, we must have a way of describing or measuring risk, and the issue is now how this should be done.

As we have seen, risk has two main dimensions – consequences and uncertainties–and a risk description is obtained by specifying the consequences and using a description (measure) of uncertainty, Q. The most common tool is probability P (subjective probability or often also referred to as judgemental and knowledge-based probability), but others exist – see Section 2.4 and Aven et al. (2014). Specifying the consequences means to identify a set of quantities of interest C' that characterise the consequences C, for example, the number of fatalities. The C's are the high-level observable quantities of the risk analysis, such as profit, production, production loss, number of fatalities, number of attacks and the occurrence of an accident. These are the quantities that we should like to know the value of at the time of the decisions since they provide information about the performance of the alternatives studied. In the risk analysis, these quantities are predicted and the uncertainties assessed. We are performing the risk analysis to provide decision support for investment, design, operation and so on, and a set of decision alternatives are being considered.

Now, depending on the principles laid down for specifying C' and the choice of Q, we obtain different perspectives on how to describe/measure risk. As a general description of risk, we can write:

Risk description $= (C', Q, K)$, (or alternatively, (A', C', Q, K), A' some specified A events),

where K is the background knowledge (models and data used, assumptions, etc.) on which Q and C' are based.

To simplify the presentation, we will normally just write C and A also when referring to specific C's and A's in the following. In the setting of a risk description, we always have in mind the specific C' and A'.

A common approach to risk assessment is to let $Q = P$, that is, knowledge-based probability is the tool used to express the uncertainties. However, this choice can be challenged; there is a need for seeing beyond the probabilities. We will return to this issue in Section 2.4. For now, unless otherwise stated, $Q = P$.

The probability is interpreted with reference to an uncertainty standard, for example, an urn (see Appendix A.1): if the assessor assigns a probability of an event A equal to say 0.1, it means that the assessor compares his/her uncertainty (degree of belief) about the occurrence of the event A with drawing a specific ball at random from an urn that contains 10 balls. To show the dependency of the background knowledge K that the probabilities are based on, we write $P(A|K)$. We may also use odds; if the probability of an event A is 0.10, the odds against A are 9:1. The assignments are based on available information and knowledge; if we had sufficient information, we would be able to predict with certainty the value of the quantities of interest. The quantities are unknown to us as we have lack of knowledge about how people would act, how machines would work and so on. Systems analysis and modelling would increase the background knowledge and thus hopefully reduce uncertainties. In some cases, however, the analysis and modelling could in fact increase our uncertainty about the future value of the unknown quantities. Think of a situation where the analyst is confident that a certain type of machine is to be used for future operation. A more detailed analysis may, however, reveal that also other machine types are being considered. And as a consequence, the analysts' uncertainty about the future performance of the system may increase. Normally, we would be far away from being able to see the future with certainty, but the principle is the important issue here; uncertainties related to the future observable quantities are epistemic, that is, they result from lack of knowledge.

Here are some more examples: the first one is linked to the health case introduced earlier.

Illness (Refer Figure 1.1)

Risk
C: The occurrence or not of specific diseases (known or unknown types) and other plagues, their time of occurrence, and their consequences for a person (John) (he may die, suffer, etc.).
U: Today we do not know if John will contract one or more of these illnesses, and we do not know what their consequences will be.

Risk description
A: John contracts a certain illness next year.
C: John's recovery time and overall health state, simplified in four categories: John recovers during the course of 1 month, 1 month − 1 year, John never recovers, John dies as a result of the illness.
P: Based on our knowledge of this illness K, we can express a probability that John contracts this illness, for example, 10%, and that if he gets the illness, the probability that he will die is 5%. We write $P(A|K) = 0.10$ and $P(\text{he dies}|A, K) = 0.05$. The symbol | is read as 'given', so that $P(A|K)$ expresses our probability that A will occur given our knowledge K.
K: the knowledge on which these assessments are based on − referred to as the background knowledge (data, information, justified beliefs, assumptions)

Dose - response

Physicians often talk about the dose–response relationship. Formulae are established showing the link between a dose and the average response. The dose here means the amount of drugs introduced into the body, the training dose and so on. This is the initiating event A. In most cases, it is known – there is no uncertainty related to A. The consequence (the response) of the dose is denoted C. It can, for instance, be a clinical symptom or another physical or pathological reaction within the body. By establishing a dose–response curve, we can determine a typical (average) response value for a specific dose. In a particular case, the response C is unknown. It is uncertain (U). How likely it is that a specific C will take different outcomes can be expressed by means of probabilities. These probabilities will be based on the available background knowledge K. We may, for example, assign a probability of 10% that the response will be a factor 2 higher than the typical (average) response value.

Exposure - health effects

Within the discipline *work environment*, one often uses the terms 'exposure' and associated 'health effects'. The exposure can, for example, be linked to biological factors (bacteria, viruses, fungi, etc.), noise and radiation. An initiating event A could be that this exposure has reached a certain magnitude. The consequences – the health effects – are denoted C, and we can repeat the presentation of the dose–response example.

Disconnection from server

Risk
C: The occurrence or non-occurrence of a computer server failure and its consequences.
U: Today we do not know whether the server will fail or not, and what the consequences will be in case of failures.

Risk description
A: The computer server fails (no longer functions) over the next 24 hours.
C: The effect on production, categorised as No consequences, reduced production speed and production stoppage.
P: We know that the server has failed many times previously. Based on the historical data (K), we assign a probability of 0.01 that the server will fail in the course of the next 24 hours. The failure of the server has never before led to a production shutdown. However, system experts assign a probability of 2% for a production shutdown in the event of a server failure. Hence, $P(A|K) = 0.01$ and $P(\text{production stoppage}|A, K) = 0.02$.
K: the background knowledge.

Fire in a road tunnel

Risk
C: The occurrence or not of a fire in the tunnel and the consequences from such a fire.

U: Today we do not know if there will be a fire in the tunnel and the consequences from such a fire.

Risk description
A: A fire breaks out in a vehicle in a certain road tunnel during the next year.
C: The losses of a fire, categorised as lightly injured road users, severely injured road users, $1 - 4$ killed, $5 - 20$ killed, more than 20 killed.
P: We establish a model that expresses the relationship between the tunnel fire and various factors, such as traffic volume, traffic type and speed limit. We use the model in combination with historical data to assign a probability 0.1% that there will be a fire in the tunnel.
K: the background knowledge.

Product sale

An enterprise that manufactures a particular product initiates a campaign to increase sales.
Risk
C: Sales (profitability)
U: Today we do not know the sales and profitability numbers.

Risk description
C: Sales quantity.
P: Based on historical knowledge (K), the probability that the sales will be less than 100 is expressed as $P(C < 100|K) = 0.05$.
K: the background knowledge.

We may rephrase the above definition of risk by saying that risk associated with an activity is to be understood as (Aven and Renn 2009a):

> *Uncertainty about and severity of the consequences of an activity*, where severity refers to intensity, size, extension, and so on, and is with respect to something that humans value (lives, the environment, money, etc). Losses and gains, for example, expressed by money or the number of fatalities, are ways of defining the severity of the consequences.

Hence, risk equals uncertainty about the consequences of an activity seen in relation to the severity of the consequences. Note that the uncertainties relate to the consequences C; the severity is just a way of characterising the consequences.

A low degree of uncertainty does not necessarily mean a low risk, or a high degree of uncertainty does not necessarily mean a high risk. Consider a case where only two outcomes are possible, 0 and 1, corresponding to 0 fatalities and 1 fatality, and the decision alternatives are I and II, having probability distributions (0.5, 0.5) and (0.0001, 0.9999), respectively. Hence, for alternative I, there is a higher degree of uncertainty than for alternative II. However, considering both dimensions, we would, of course, judge alternative II to have the highest risk as the negative outcome 1 is nearly certain to occur.

If uncertainty U is replaced by probability P, we can define risk as follows:

> Probabilities associated with the consequences of the activity, seen in relation to the severity of these consequences.

In the example above, (0.5, 0.5) and (0.0001, 0.9999) are the probabilities (probability distributions) related to the outcomes 0 and 1. Here, the outcome 1 means a high severity, and a judgement about the risk being high would give weight to the probability that the outcome will be 1.

However, in general, we cannot replace uncertainty U by probability P. This is an important point. The main argument is that probability is just a tool to express our uncertainty with respect to C, and this tool is 'imperfect'. We can have poor knowledge about a phenomena, but judge the probability of a related undesirable event to be small, say 0.01. Would we then give this probability much weight in a decision-making context? Probably not, as the knowledge supporting the probability is so weak. Uncertainties may in fact be hidden in the background knowledge, K. For example, you may assign a probability of fatalities occurring on an offshore installation based on the assumption that the installation structure will withstand a certain accidental load. In real life, the structure could however fail at a lower load level. The probability did not reflect this uncertainty. Risk analyses are always based on a number of such assumptions.

The event A in (A, C, U) is referred to as a hazard or a threat. It is common to link hazards to accidental events (safety) and threats to intentional acts (security).

The event A can also be associated with an opportunity. An example is a shutdown of a production system, which allows for preventive maintenance.

In a risk description we often add C^*, a prediction of C. By a prediction, we mean a forecast of which value this quantity will take in real life. In the product sale example, we would like to predict the sales. We may use one number, but often we specify a prediction interval $[a, b]$ such that C will be in the interval with a certain probability (typical 90% or 95%). In the illness example, our focus will be on prediction of the consequence C, given that the event A has occurred, i.e., the time it takes to recover. Experience shows that on average it takes 1 month for recovery, and then we can use this as a prediction of the consequence C.

Using a number such as this is problematic, however, as the uncertainty about the consequence C is often large. It is more informative to use a prediction interval or formulate probabilities for various consequence categories of C, for example: the person will recover within 10 days, the person will recover within 1 month, the person will never recover or the person will die. We will return to such descriptions in Section 2.3.

2.2   Vulnerability

A concept closely related to risk is vulnerability. It is basically risk conditional on the occurrence of an event A.

Let us return to the illness example in Chapter 1. If the person (John) contracts the illness, that is, A occurs, what will be the consequences then? It depends on how vulnerable he is. He may be young, old, physically strong or already weakened before contracting the illness. We use the concept vulnerability when we are concerned about the consequences, given that an event (in this case, the illness) has occurred. As mentioned earlier, we often refer to this event as an initiating event. Looking into the future, the consequences are not known, and vulnerability is then to be understood as the combination of consequences and the associated uncertainty, that is, $(C, U \mid A)$, using the notation introduced earlier.

The vulnerability description takes the general form $(C', Q, K | A)$, given A.

When we say that a system is vulnerable, we mean that the vulnerability is considered to be high.

If we know that the person is already in a weakened state of health prior to the illness, we can say that the vulnerability is high. There is a high probability that the patient will die.

Vulnerability is an aspect of risk. Because of this, the vulnerability analysis is a part of the risk analysis. If vulnerability is highlighted in the analysis, we often talk about risk and vulnerability analyses.

2.3   How to describe risk quantitatively

As explained earlier, a description of risk contains the following components (Q, K). How are these quantities described? We have already provided a number of examples of how we express Q, but here we will take a step further. We consider two areas of application, economics and safety. But first we recall the definition of the expected value, EX, of an unknown quantity, X, for example, expressing costs or the number of fatalities. Here X is an example of using the above terminology. If X can assume three values, say $-10, 0$ and 100, with respective probabilities of $0.1, 0.6$ and 0.3, then the expected value of X is

$$EX = (-10) \cdot 0.1 + 0 \cdot 0.6 + 100 \cdot 0.3 = 29.$$

We interpret EX as the centre of gravity of the probability distribution for X. See Appendix A.1.

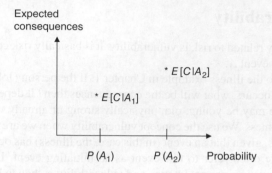

Figure 2.1   Risk description for two events A_1 and A_2, with associated expectations $E[C|A_1]$ and $E[C|A_2]$.

Imagine a situation where we are faced with two possible initiating events A_1 and A_2, for example, two illnesses. Should these events occur, we would expect consequences $E[C|A_1]$ and $E[C|A_2]$, respectively. If we compare these expected values with the probabilities for A_1 and A_2, we obtain a simple way of expressing the risk, as shown in Figure 2.1. If the event's position (marked *) is located in the far right of the figure, the risk is considered high, and if the event is located in the far left, the risk as described by these dimensions is low.

An alternative risk description is obtained by focusing on the possible consequences or consequence categories, instead of the expected consequences. We return to the illness example, where we defined the following consequence categories:

C_1: The person recovers in 1 month

C_2: The person recovers in 1 month − 1 year

C_3: The person never recovers

C_4: The person dies as a result of the illness

For illness A_1, we can then establish a description as shown in Figure 2.2. Here $P(C_1)$ expresses the probability that the person contracts the actual illness and recovers within 1 month, that is, $P(C_1) = P(A_1$ and $C_1)$. We interpret the other probabilities in a similar manner.

Alternatively, we may assume that the analysis is carried out conditional on the event that the person is already ill, and $P(C_1)$ then expresses the probability that the person will recover in a month. In this case, $P(C_1)$ is to be read as $P(C_1|A_1)$.

It is common to use categories also for the probability dimension, and the risk description of Figure 2.2 can alternatively be presented as in Figure 2.3. We refer to the figure (matrix) as a risk matrix. We see that the use of such matrices could make it difficult to distinguish between various risks since it is based on rather crude categories.

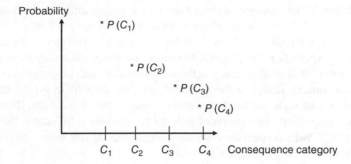

Figure 2.2   Risk description based on four consequence categories.

Consequences Probability	C_1	C_2	C_3	C_4
Highly probable Higher than 50%	x			
Probable 10% − 50%		x		
Low probability 10% − 2%			x	x
Unlikely Less than 2%				

Figure 2.3   Example of a risk matrix. The x in column C_1 shows that there is a probability greater than 0.5 for consequence C_1. The numbers are conditional that the person is ill.

Often a logarithmic or an approximately logarithmic scale is used on the probability axis. Risk matrices can be set up for different attributes, for example, with respect to economic quantities and loss of lives. We present a number of examples of risk matrices throughout the book. We also provide an in-depth discussion of the method. The reader is referred to Section 13.3.2.

2.3.1   Description of risk in a financial context

An enterprise is considering making an investment, and we denote the value of the return on this investment next year by X. Since X is unknown, we are led to predictions of X and uncertainty assessments (using probabilities). Instead of expressing the entire probability distribution of X, it is common to use a measure of central tendency, normally the expectation, together with a measure of variation/volatility, normally taken as the variance, standard deviation or a quantile of the distribution, for example, the 90% quantile v, which is defined by $P(X \le v) = 0.90$.

Based on average returns in the market for this type of investments, the enterprise establishes an expectation (prediction). However, the actual value may show a significant deviation from this value, and it is the deviation that one is especially concerned about in this context. Risk and the risk analysis have their focus on the uncertainties viewed in relation to the market average values. The variance and the quantiles thus become important expressions of risk. In the economic literature, the concept 'Value-at-Risk' (VaR) is often used for such a quantile. A VaR with a confidence of 90% is equal to the 90% quantile v.

2.3.2   Description of risk in a safety context

In a safety context, terms such as 'FAR', 'PLL', 'IR', and 'F-N-curve' are commonly used. We will explain these terms below.

In situations where risk is focused on loss of lives, the FAR (Fatal Accident Rate) value is often used to describe the level of risk.

The FAR value is defined as the expected loss of life per 100 million (10^8) hours of exposure.

When the FAR concept was introduced, 10^8 hours corresponded to the time of 1000 persons present at their workplace through a full life span. Today it takes 1400 persons to reach 100 million working hours. The FAR value is often related to various categories of activities or personnel. Such activity- or personnel-related FAR values are usually more informative than average values.

The expected number of fatalities over a year is referred to as PLL (Potential Loss of Life).

If we assume that there are n persons exposed to a risk for t hours per year, the connection between PLL and FAR can be expressed by the following formula:

$$FAR = [PLL/nt]10^8.$$

The average probability of dying in an accident for n persons, referred to as the AIR (Average Individual Risk), can be expressed as

$$AIR = PLL/n.$$

Another form of risk description is associated with the so-called safety functions. Examples of such functions are

- preventing escalation of accident situations so that personnel outside the immediate accident area are not injured;

- maintaining the capacity of main load-bearing structures until the facility has been evacuated;

- protecting rooms of significance to combatting accidents so that they remain operative until the facility has been evacuated;

- protecting the facility's safe areas so that they remain intact until the facility has been evacuated;

- maintaining at least one escape route from every area where personnel are found until evacuation to the facility's safe areas and rescue of personnel have been completed.

Risk associated with loss of a safety function is expressed by the probability, or the frequency, of events in which this safety function is impaired. This form of risk description has its origin in analysis of offshore installations and is especially useful in the design phase.

In many cases, crude categories are used for both probability and consequences, as illustrated in the risk matrix (Figure 2.4).

An alternative categorisation based on probability for a given year is shown in Figure 2.3.

An F–N curve (Frequency–Number of Fatalities) is an alternative way of describing the risk associated with loss of lives; refer to Figure 2.5. An F–N curve shows the frequency of accident events with at least N fatalities, where the axes are normally logarithmic. The F–N curve describes the risk related to large-scale accidents and is thus especially suited for characterising societal risk.

In a similar way, accident frequencies for personal injuries, environmental spills, loss of material goods and so on can be defined.

Consequences Probability	Insigni-ficant	Small Non-serious injuries	Moderate Serious injuries	Large Serious injuries 1 – 2 fatalities	Very large More than 2 fatalities
Highly probable Less than 1 year					
Probable 1 – 10 years					
Low probability 10 – 50 years					
Unlikely 50 years or more					

Figure 2.4   Example of a risk matrix. The category 'Unlikely' corresponds to a prediction of one event in 50 years or more, 'Low probability' corresponds to a prediction of one event in 10–50 years and so on.

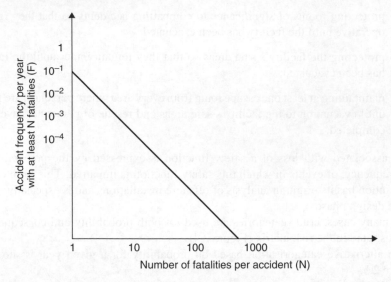

Figure 2.5   Example of an F–N curve (Frequency–Number of fatalities).

Note that frequency is an average number of events per unit of time or per operation. The connection between frequency and probability is illustrated by the following example. Assume that for a specific company we have calculated the frequency of accidents leading to personnel injuries, at 7 per year, that is, $7/8760 = 0.0008$ per hour. From this rate, we may assign a probability of 0.0008 that such an accident will occur during 1 hour. This approach for transforming frequencies to probabilities works when this value is small – how small depends on the desired accuracy. As a rule of thumb, one often uses 'less than 0.10'.

It is also common to talk about observed (historical) PLL (number of fatalities per year) values, FAR (the number of fatalities per 100 million exposure hours) values and so on.

Various normalisations may be used depending on the application involved. For example, in a vehicular transport context, we are primarily concerned with the (expected) number of fatalities and injuries per kilometre and year.

2.4   Qualitative judgements

First let us again reflect on why we need to see beyond probability to express risk. A probability expresses the degree of belief concerning the occurrence of an event given some background knowledge. Suppose that a probability equal to 0.5 is assigned in a particular case. This value can be based on strong or weak background knowledge, in the sense that in one case there is a significant amount of relevant data and/or other information and knowledge that supports a value of 0.50, while, in another case, few or no data or other information/knowledge support this value. Let us look at an extreme case. You hold a normal coin and throw it. You specify a probability of 0.50 for observing a head – the background knowledge is strong. The probability judgement is based on the argument that both sides are equally likely because of symmetry, and experience of such coins supports getting a head in roughly 50% of throws. But let us imagine that you are to assign the probability of a new coin that you know nothing about, it can be normal or abnormal (you will not see it). What is then your probability? You will most probably still say 50%. But now the background knowledge is weak. You have little insight into what kind of coin this is. We see that we get the same probability, but the background knowledge in the former case is strong and weak in the latter case. When assessing the 'strength' of an assigned probability, it is clearly important to also consider the background knowledge. The number alone does not say much. This is the situation when we use probabilities to describe the risk. The figures are based on background knowledge, and we must some know how strong this is to use the numbers in the right way in the risk management. The following aspects have to be considered: How good are the data and models that support the probability judgements? What about the expert opinions included? And all the assumptions made – how reasonable are they?

Hence, standard risk matrices must be used with care. We must be aware that they have clear limitations in terms of providing a picture of the risk associated with an activity and that one cannot use them to draw conclusions about what is acceptable risk and what is not. For an assignment of the probability and consequences of an event, the strength of the underlying knowledge could be strong or weak, but it is not possible to see this from the probability figures alone. One can conveniently highlight the events where the background knowledge is relatively weak, so that one is particularly careful to draw conclusions on the basis of probability assignments of such events. See the illustration in Figure 2.6.

To assess this strength, a score system with three categories as suggested by Flage and Aven (2009) could, for example, be used:

The knowledge is weak if one or more of these conditions are true:

- The assumptions made represent strong simplifications.

- Data/information are non-existent or highly unreliable/irrelevant.

- There is strong disagreement among experts.

- The phenomena involved are poorly understood, models are non-existent or known/believed to give poor predictions.

Consequences Probability	Insigi-ficant	Small (Non-serious injuries)	Moderate (Serious injuries)	Large (Serious injuries 1 − 2 fatalities)	Very large (>2 fatalities)
Highly probable (<1 year)					
Probable (1 − 10 years)		•			
Low probability (10 − 50 years)			∘		
Unlikely (50 years or more)				◊	

Figure 2.6   Example of a risk matrix, where the assignments are supported by strong, medium and weak background knowledge. Strong knowledge: •, medium strong knowledge: ∘: and weak knowledge: ◊.

If, on the other hand, all (whenever they are relevant) of the following conditions are met, the knowledge is considered strong:

1. The assumptions made are seen as very reasonable.

2. Large amount of reliable and relevant data/information are available.

3. There is a broad agreement among experts.

4. The phenomena involved are well understood; the models used are known to give predictions with the required accuracy.

Cases in between are classified as having a medium strength of knowledge.

A simplified version of these criteria is obtained by using the same score for strong but give the medium and weak scores for a suitable number of conditions not met, for example, medium if one or two of the conditions 1–4 are not met and the is score weak otherwise, that is, when three or four of the conditions are not met.

The strength illustrated in the risk matrix could be shown by coloured events, for example, red (dark), yellow (dashed) or green (light), depending on whether the background knowledge is considered to be weak, medium or strong, respectively, or as illustrated in Figure 2.6: Strong knowledge: •; medium strong knowledge: ∘ and weak knowledge: ◊.

An alternative approach is presented by Aven (2013d) for assessing the strength of knowledge of K, by assessing the risk associated with deviations from the assumptions made (assumption deviation risk).

The quantitative analysis can be supplemented in many other ways, for example, by introducing a red team (devil's advocate) addressing issues such as the following:

- Searching for unknown knowns, that is, events that are known by others, but not by the original analysis group
- Arguing for the occurrence of events that are considered to have negligible probability
- Checking that relevant signals and warnings have been properly reflected.

The point is to challenge the judgements and assumptions made in the quantitative analysis.

3

The risk analysis process: planning

In this chapter, we discuss the planning of a risk analysis including the risk evaluation, that is, the risk assessment. The activity can be divided into the following two sub-activities; refer Figure 1.2:

- Problem definition, information gathering and organisation of work (we refer to this as the problem definition activity)

- Selection of analysis method.

3.1 Problem definition

The first step of a risk analysis is to define the objectives of the analysis. Why should we perform the analysis? Often, the objectives are based on a problem definition, as shown by the following example.

Example

A manufacturing company conducts a series of tests everyday on its products and then stores the information in an Information and Communication Technology (ICT) system (called system S) that automatically adjusts the production process at start-up the next day. If this information is erroneous, a large quantity of products may not meet the quality requirements and hence cannot be released into the market. This will result in significant economic losses. If system S fails, production must be stopped,

Risk Analysis, Second Edition. Terje Aven.
© 2015 John Wiley & Sons, Ltd. Published 2015 by John Wiley & Sons, Ltd.

again causing economic losses. To improve the reliability of system S, management has decided to conduct a risk analysis with the following objective:

– Based on a risk analysis of system S, addressing 'failure of system S' and 'erroneous information', propose and recommend suitable risk-reducing measures.

When formulating the objectives, any limitations to the scope of the analysis must be taken into consideration, such as lack of available resources, time limits and lack of data and information. This is necessary in order to balance the complexity and size of the problem on the one hand, with the scope, ambitions and accuracy of the analysis on the other.

Clear boundaries for the analysis must be made, so that there is no doubt about what the results apply to. The operating conditions that are to be included in the analysis must also be determined. Examples of different operating conditions are start-up, normal operation, testing, maintenance and emergency situations.

A working group must be established. This group must have knowledge about risk analysis and the system. Other types of specialised competence, for example, in mathematical statistics, will be required in some cases.

A plan for the risk analysis should be drawn up. The plan should cover activities, responsibilities, work progress, time limits and milestones, reports and budget.

The risk analysis may address different types of attributes, such as life, health, environment, economic quantities, information and services. If several attributes are to be analysed, it must be determined whether they are to be analysed separately or they are to be combined in some way.

Experience shows that focus is often placed on the risk analysis in itself, including analysis of data and risk calculations and less on the planning and the use of the analyses. A more balanced analysis process will be achieved if we distribute the resources more evenly. A rule of thumb is that we should use one-third of the resources for planning, one-third for the risk analysis and evaluation and one-third for the risk treatment.

It is essential that we make it clear how the analyses are to be used in the decision-making process. The use, to a large extent, determines the risk analysis approach and methods. The interested parties must also be identified, so that the analysis can be suited to these parties.

Here are some examples on how the analysis can be used in the decision-making process:

• *Consider changes in the risk*: An analysis of the risk-reducing effect of the different alternatives or measures. The risk analysis may show, for example, that a particular measure reduces the risk by 2%, while another reduces the risk by 10%. This can in itself produce clear recommendations on what is a sensible strategy going forward, if the costs for the measures are about the same.

- *Cost-effectiveness*: In the cost-effectiveness analysis, indices such as the expected cost per expected number of lives saved are calculated. If a measure costs 2 million euros and the risk analysis shows that the measure will bring about a reduction in the number of expected fatalities by 0.1, then this cost-effectiveness index would be equal to $2/0.1 = 20$ million euros. This quantity is often referred to as the *implied value of a statistical life* or the *Implied Cost of Averting a Fatality* (ICAF). By comparing this number with reference values, we can assess the effectiveness of the measure. This type of ratio (index) can also be calculated in relation to quantities other than life, for example, a ton of spilled oil. Empirical studies of implemented measures show large differences when it comes to the value of an implied statistical life.

- *Cost-benefit analysis*: Cost-benefit analysis is an approach to measure benefits and costs of a project. The common scale used to measure benefits and costs is currency of the country. After transforming all attributes to monetary values, the total performance is summarised by computing the expected net present value, the $E[NPV]$. The main principle in transformation of goods into monetary values is to find out the maximum amount society is willing to pay to obtain a specific benefit. Use of cost-benefit analysis is considered as a tool for obtaining efficient allocation of the resources, by identifying which potential actions are worth undertaking and in what way. According to this approach, a measure should be implemented if the expected net present value is positive, that is, if $E[NPV] > 0$. Although cost-benefit analysis was originally developed for the evaluation of public policy issues, it is also used in other contexts, in particular, for evaluating projects in firms. The same methods can be applied by using values reflecting the decision-maker's benefits and costs and the decision-maker's willingness to pay. To measure the NPV of a project, the relevant project cash flows (the movement of money into and out of the business) are specified, and the time value of money is taken into account by discounting future cash flows by the appropriate rate of return. The formula used to calculate NPV is as follows:

$$NPV = \sum_{t=0}^{n} \frac{a_t}{(1 + i)^t},\qquad (3.1)$$

where a_t represents the cash flow at time t and i is the discount rate. The terms capital cost and alternative cost are also used for i. As these terms express, i represents the investor's cost related to not employing the capital in alternative investments. When considering projects where the cash flows are known in advance, the rate of return associated with other risk-free investments, such as bank deposits, makes the basis for the discount rate to be used in the NPV calculations. When the cash flows are uncertain, which is usually the case, they are normally represented by their expected values $E[a_t]$, and the rate of return is increased on the basis of the Capital Asset Pricing Model (CAPM) in order to outweigh the possibilities of unfavourable outcomes. Not all types of uncertainties are considered relevant when determining the magnitude of the risk-adjusted discount rate, as shown by the portfolio theory; see for example Levy and Sarnat (1990). This theory justifies the ignorance of unsystematic risk and states that the only relevant risk is the systematic risk associated with a project. The systematic risk relates to general market movements, for example, caused by political events, and the unsystematic risk relates to specific project uncertainties, for example, accident risks. The method implies transformation of goods into monetary values, for example using the value of a 'statistical life'. What is the maximum amount the society (or the decision-maker) is willing to pay to reduce the expected number of fatalities by 1? Typical numbers for the value of a statistical life used in cost-benefit analysis are 1–10 million euros. The Ministry of Finance in Norway has arrived at a value at approximately 3.5 million euros. For official cost-benefit analyses, the Ministry of Finance recommends the use of a value of this order of magnitude. An oil company uses the following guideline values for the cost to avert a statistical life (euros):

0	Highly effective, always implement
10,000	Effective, always implement
0.1 million	Effective; implement unless individual risk is negligible
1 million	Consider; effective if individual risk levels are high
10 million	Consider at high individual risk levels or when there are other benefits
100 million	Not socially effective – look at other options

- *Risk acceptance criteria (risk tolerability limits)*: If the calculated risk is lower than a pre-determined value, then the risk is acceptable (tolerable). Otherwise, the risk is unacceptable (intolerable), and risk-reducing measures are required. One example of such a criterion is the following: the frequency of events during 1 year that leads to impairment of a safety function must not exceed $1 \cdot 10^{-4}$. If the risk analysis arrives at a calculated frequency higher than this limit, then the risk is unacceptable, and if the frequency is lower, then the risk is acceptable. We refer to Chapter 5.

- *ALARP process*: The risk should be reduced to a level that is As Low As Reasonably Practicable (ALARP). This principle means that the benefits of a measure should be assessed in relation to the disadvantages or costs of the measure. The ALARP principle is based on 'reversed burden of proof', which means that an identified measure should be implemented unless it cannot be documented that there is an unreasonable disparity ('gross disproportion') between costs/disadvantages and benefits.

One way of assessing 'gross disproportion' is outlined in what follows (Aven and Vinnem 2005, 2007):

1. Perform a crude analysis of the benefits and burdens of the various alternatives, addressing attributes related to feasibility, conformance with good practice, economy, strategy considerations, risk, robustness/resilience, social responsibility and so on. The analysis would typically be qualitative and its conclusions summarised in a matrix with performance shown by a simple categorisation system such as very positive, positive, neutral, negative, very negative. From this crude analysis, a decision can be made to eliminate some alternatives and include new ones for further detailing and analysis. Frequently, such crude analyses give the necessary platform for choosing one appropriate alternative. When considering a set of possible risk-reducing measures, a qualitative analysis in many cases provides a sufficient basis for identifying which measures to implement, as these measures are in accordance with good engineering or good operational practice. Also many measures can be quickly eliminated as the qualitative analysis reveals that the burdens are much more dominant than the benefits. If the costs are small, the ALARP principle would imply that an identified measure improving the safety should be implemented.

2. From this crude analysis, the need for further analyses is determined, to give a better basis for concluding which alternative(s) to choose. This may include various types of risk analyses.

3. Other types of analyses may be conducted to assess, for example, costs and indices such as expected cost per expected number of saved lives could be computed to provide information about the effectiveness of a risk-reducing measure or compare various alternatives. The expected net present value may also be computed when found appropriate. Sensitivity analyses should be performed to see the effects of varying values of statistical lives and other key parameters. Often the conclusions are rather straightforward when calculating indices such as the expected cost per expected number of saved lives over the field life and the expected cost per expected averted ton of oil spill over the field life. If a conclusion about gross disproportion is not clear, then these measures and alternatives are clear candidates for implementation. Clearly, if a risk-reducing measure has a positive expected net present value (for suitable statistical life values), it should be implemented. Crude calculations of expected net present values, ignoring difficult judgements about valuation of possible loss of lives and damage to the environment, will often be sufficient to conclude whether this criterion could justify the implementation of a measure.

4. An analysis of uncertainties in the underlying phenomena and processes is carried out. The key issue is to assess the degree for which the predicted values in the analysis (e.g. the expected costs) will deviate from the actual values (e.g. the

costs). The strength of knowledge assessment as outlined in Section 2.4 could provide useful inputs to this analysis. The alternatives are assessed with respect to their robustness/resilience, in particular, their ability to cope with surprising events occurring. See Section 5.1.1.

5. An analysis of manageability takes place. To what extent is it possible to control and reduce the uncertainties and thereby arrive at the desired outcome? Some risks are more manageable than others in the sense that there is a greater potential to reduce risk. An alternative can have a relatively high calculated risk under certain conditions, but the manageability could be good and could result in a far better outcome than expected.

6. An analysis of other factors, such as risk perception and reputation, should be carried out whenever relevant, although it may be difficult to describe how these factors would affect the standard indices used in economy and risk analysis to measure performance.

7. A total evaluation of the results of the analyses should be performed, to summarise the pros and cons of the various alternatives, where considerations of the constraints and limitations of the analyses are also taken into account. A risk-reducing measure may not be justified by reference to the cost-benefit type of analysis, but if it contributes strongly to increased robustness/resilience, it may still be recommended for implementation.

Note that such assessments are not necessarily limited to the ALARP processes. The above process can also be used in other contexts where decisions are to be made under uncertainty.

Different checklists can be established for the identification of such uncertainty factors (see Chapters 4 and 5).

3.2   Selection of analysis method

The selection of analysis method can be made based on the following considerations:

- To what extent do we want or need a simplified, standard or model-based method? See Table 1.1. This depends on the aim of the analysis.

- To what extent are branch-specific methods available?

- Which parts of the risk picture in Figure 1.1 are to be emphasised? Various methods have different focus.

An experienced risk analyst will often base the selection of method on previous analyses. He/she has extensive knowledge of the various risk analysis methods and knows how they should be used in practice. In many instances, however, it is not obvious which method should be used. New analysts arrive on the scene, and they need guidance regarding the method selection.

In the following sections, two example procedures are presented (checklist-based procedure and risk-based procedure) that may be used to select the type of risk analysis method: simplified, standard or model-based. When the type of risk analysis method has been selected, one can choose an appropriate method within this category. The choice depends on the phase, ease of access to information, the system's significance, the system's complexity and other factors.

Often, several risk analyses are implemented in sequence. For example, a simplified analysis is used to identify critical systems. After this, a standard or possibly a model-based analysis may be carried out to analyse these systems in more detail and to form a basis for recommending risk-reducing measures.

The selection of analysis method is also about choosing between a forward and a backward approach:

- *Forward approach*: The risk analysis begins with the identification of initiating events. Thereafter, the consequences of the various events are analysed. The aim of the analysis is to identify all relevant events and associated scenarios. For example, if we analyse a process module on an offshore installation or a land-based facility, the aim is to identify all gas leakages that can occur. After this, a consequence analysis is carried out for each initiating event, addressing possible explosion and fire scenarios leading to possible loss of safety functions and fatalities. The same will be done for all other types of events that are possible in this area, for example, dropped objects. The end product will be a risk analysis that describes both insignificant and severe events, with their associated potential consequences.

- *Backward approach*: In this case, the risk analysis begins with the identification of the resulting events or situations that are identified as important in the analysis, for example, the impairment of escape routes, personnel injuries or loss of lives. In the case of a process module, we will be concerned with the identification of potential fire situations that can block an escape route. What kind of a fire can result in impairment of the escape route? Where must it occur and how large must it be? What leakage sources can result in such a large fire? The end product will be a limited analysis that looks into some selected events capable of affecting the performance measures highlighted in the analysis.

Generally, one can say that the backward approach is less resource intensive in terms of time, but at the same time, it requires considerable experience and competence, in order for the analysis to provide a good basis for decision-making. There is a danger that one could make a wrong choice or overlook events that should have been included.

The forward approach implies more mechanised and time-consuming calculation processes. The risk description may in this case be more complete, but there is a

Table 3.1   Example of a checklist for selection of analysis method – road tunnels.

Tunnel type	Gradient	Length (km)	Simplified risk analysis	Standard risk analysis	Model-based risk analysis
One or two-run tunnels	0.5%	0.5–1.0	x		
		1.0–5.0	x	x	
		>5.0	x		x
	>5%	0.5–1.0	x	x	
		>1.0	x		x
Undersea tunnels	0–10%	Regardless of length	x		x
On- and off-ramps in tunnel	Regardless of gradient	Regardless of length	x		x

danger that the risk analysis becomes so extensive and complicated that it is difficult to extract what information is important and what is less important. We may spend too much time on aspects that do not contribute to risk.

3.2.1   Checklist-based approach

In this section, we present a checklist-based approach for selecting a risk analysis method. A road tunnel example is used to illustrate the approach. The description is, to a large extent, based on the Norwegian Public Roads Administration (2007). See Table 3.1.

We see from the table that there are three conditions that form the basis for the selection of method: tunnel type, gradient and length. Other conditions can also affect the selection of method, for example:

- traffic volume;
- the project phase (planning/design, under construction, existing tunnels);
- special constructions (intersection layouts, roundabouts, on- and off-ramps);
- danger of water ingress;
- special technical arrangements;
- local climatic conditions;

- high proportion of heavy motor vehicles;

- transportation of dangerous goods;

- high speed levels observed in relation to posted speed limits;

- special preparedness-related conditions (long response time, poor access to water);

- special conditions related to the traffic picture (e.g. high traffic periods of the week or day).

Depending on such conditions, the category method may be adjusted.

From the checklist in Table 3.1, we see that several categories of methods are applicable in certain situations. For example, both simplified and model-based risk analyses will be applicable for undersea tunnels. Initially, a simplified analysis can be undertaken to perform a crude risk analysis and to decide what the focus should be in a subsequent model-based risk analysis method.

3.2.2   Risk-based approach

This section gives a brief description of the principles of a risk-based approach for the selection of a risk analysis method. The approach is based on Wiencke et al. (2006). The method was initially developed for the ICT industry, but can also be applied to other analysis subjects.

This approach is based on an assessment of the following three aspects:

1. *Expected consequences*, computed by multiplying the probability that a specific initiating event occurs and the expected consequence if this event occurs. The consequences are often related to the degree of non-conformance with the objectives of the organisation.

2. *Uncertainties* related to factors that can create deviations/surprises relative to the expected values. Important factors that can lead to such deviations/surprises could be both variation and lack of knowledge, for example, due to the complexity of the technology or the organisation, availability of information, time frame for the analysis.

3. *Frame conditions*, that is, limitations with respect to budget, time period and access to information.

This approach builds, in principle, on an overall risk assessment in that items 1 and 2 express risk. The assessment is crude, as the point here is not to conduct a risk assessment, but to provide a basis for selecting an adequate risk analysis method. The assessment is expected to take a few hours. It can be carried out by the system owner (e.g. the project leader), with support from risk analysts and persons with comprehensive knowledge of the system or activity being analysed.

Assessing each of these three main points is based on simple questionnaires. See Appendix C for further details.

Reflection

Is it a reasonable demand that the choice of analysis method be justified?

Yes, in that the choice of analysis method can influence the form and content of the risk picture that is to be presented. On the other hand, the resource consumption linked to selection and documentation must not be too high. The aim of the approach in Appendix C is to balance these concerns.

Reflection

Many risk analyses use statistics as a starting point for the analysis. Which analysis type does such an analysis fall under: simplified, standard or model-based risk analysis?

All three categories can be relevant. The method depends on how the statistics are applied. Let us look at the yearly number of road traffic fatalities in a specific country.

This is a description of what has happened, so the numbers are not expressing risk as such (refer 'Reflection' in Chapter 1). However, when we address the future, for example, by looking at the number of fatalities next year, the risk concept is introduced – unknown events and consequences, and associated uncertainties.

A simplified risk analysis can conclude that one expects a reduction in fatalities in the coming years. This conclusion can be based on a discussion within the analysis working group, where the statistics are an important part of the background knowledge.

A standard risk analysis can, for example, express a 90% prediction interval $[a, b]$ for the number of fatalities X next year, which means that $P(a \leq X \leq b) = 0.90$. An expectation of the number of fatalities for the next year can be based on the previous year's statistics.

A model-based risk analysis can express the same form of results as a standard risk analysis, but makes use of more detailed models and methods. For example, the number of accidents can be described using a Poisson distribution (refer Appendix A.1). This allows the analysts to systematically study how a risk is influenced by various factors. A qualitative judgement of the strength of knowledge supporting the quantification should always be given.

4

The risk analysis process: risk assessment

In this chapter, we look closer into the different activities of a risk assessment, covering identification of initiating events, cause analysis, consequence analysis as well as risk description (risk picture); refer Figure 1.2.

4.1 Identification of initiating events

The first step of the execution part of a risk analysis is identification of initiating events. If our focus is on hazards (threats), then we are talking about a hazard identification (threat identification). It is often said that 'what you have not identified, you cannot deal with'. It is difficult to avoid or to reduce the consequences of events that one has not identified. For this reason, identification of initiating events is a critical task of the analysis. However, care has to be taken to prevent this task from becoming a routine. When one performs similar types of analyses, it is common to copy the list of hazards and threats from previous analyses. By doing this, one may overlook special aspects and features of the system being considered.

It is therefore important that identification of initiating events be carried out in a structured and systematic manner and it involves persons having the necessary competence. Figure 4.1 illustrates how such an activity can be carried out with respect to hazard identification.

Several methods are available for carrying out such an identification process, and in Figure 4.1 various techniques/methods that can be used are listed. Failure Modes and Effects Analysis (FMEA), Hazard and Operability study (HAZOP) and Structured What-If Technique (SWIFT) are discussed in Chapter 6. A common feature of all these methods is that they are based on a type of structured brainstorming in which one uses checklists, guidewords and so on adapted to the problem being studied.

Risk Analysis, Second Edition. Terje Aven.
© 2015 John Wiley & Sons, Ltd. Published 2015 by John Wiley & Sons, Ltd.

Input   **Process**   **Output**

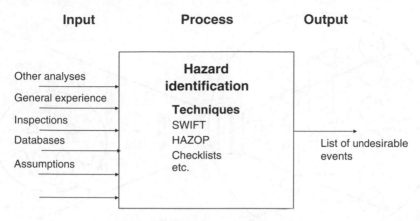

Figure 4.1   Hazard identification.

The hazard identification process should be a creative process wherein one also attempts to identify 'unusual events'. Here, as in many other instances, a form of the 80–20 rule applies, i.e., it takes 20% of the time to come up with 80% of the hazards – events that we are familiar with and have experienced – while it takes 80% of the time to arrive at the remaining hazards and threats – the unusual and not-experienced events. It is to capture some of these last-mentioned events that it is so important to adopt a systematic and structured method.

4.2   Cause analysis

In the cause analysis, we study what is needed for the initiating events to occur. What are the causal factors? Several techniques exist for this purpose, from brainstorming sessions to fault tree analyses and Bayesian networks (see Chapter 6). In Figure 4.2, we have shown an example using fault trees. Experts on the systems and activities being studied are usually necessary to carry out the analysis. An in-depth understanding of the system is normally required.

In many cases, the analysis will consist of several 'sub-risk analyses'. Let us return to the example 'Disconnection from server' discussed in Chapter 2. In the example, four different causes of the event 'disconnection from server' are identified. We look closer at one of them: power supply failure. For this new initiating event, we carry out a 'new' risk analysis. We study the causes and consequences, and a new bow-tie is established, as shown in Figure 4.3. In the consequence analysis, we are concerned with the consequences for the server, but the analysis will reveal consequences for other systems as well. This could provide a basis for assessing the need for measures that could reduce the probability of server failure, for example, labelling of cables and procedures for excavation and maintenance, or reduce the consequences of the event, for example, redundancy or having more in-lines following different routings.

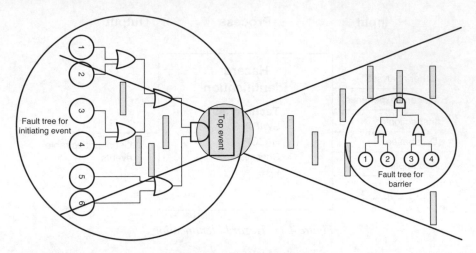

Figure 4.2   Use of fault trees.

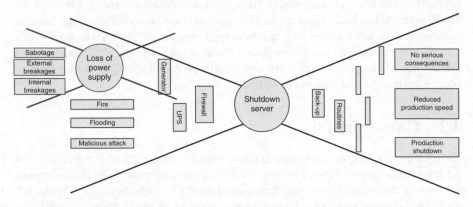

Figure 4.3   Cause analysis for disconnection from server (shutdown).

If we have access to failure data, then these can be used as a basis for predicting the number of times an event will occur. Such predictions can also be produced by using analysis methods such as fault tree analysis and Bayesian networks. If, for example, a fault tree analysis is used, one can assign probabilities for the various events in the tree (basic events), and based on the model and the assigned probabilities, the probability for the initiating event can be calculated (see Section 6.6).

4.3   Consequence analysis

For each initiating event, an analysis is carried out addressing the possible conse-quences the event can lead to. See the right side of Figure 4.3. An initiating event can often result in consequences of varying dimensions or attributes, for example, financial loss, loss of lives and environmental damage. The event tree analysis is the most common method for analysing the consequences. It will be thoroughly described in Section 6.7.

The number of steps in the event sequence is dependent on the number of barriers in the system. The aim of the consequence-reducing barriers is to prevent the initiating events from resulting in serious consequences. For each of these barriers, we can carry out barrier failure analysis and study the effect of measures taken. The fault tree analysis is often used for this purpose (see Figure 4.2). In the figure, the fault tree analysis is also used to analyse the causes triggering the initiating event.

Analyses of interdependencies between the various systems and barriers constitute an important part of the analysis. As an example, imagine that sensitive information is stored in an ICT system behind two password-protected security levels. Thus, an unauthorised user cannot gain access to the information even if he/she has access to the 'outer' security level. However, the user may find it impractical to remember many passwords, and he/she might therefore choose to use the same password for both security levels. An unauthorised user can then gain access to the sensitive information by using just one password. In this case, a dependency exists between the barriers (the same password). A solution for making the system more robust could be to make it impossible for a user to assign the same password for both security levels.

The consequence analysis deals, to a large extent, with understanding physical phenomena, and various types of models of the phenomena are used. Let us look at an example related to the initiating event 'gas leakage' on an offshore installation. These are some of the questions we will then try to answer:

- How will the gas dispersion be on the installation? In order to answer this question, we use gas dispersion models that simulate the gas under various wind and ventilation conditions, leakage rates and so on.

- Will the gas form a combustible mixture? Will a combustible gas mixture reach an ignition source? Will the gas ignite? Will there be an explosion or a fire? The models used to study these questions take into account the location and number of ignition sources, such as pumps and compressors, and are based on the results from the gas dispersion models.

- How will a possible fire develop? In order to answer this question, the so-called CFD (Computational Fluid Dynamics) simulation is often used, which predicts the spread of a fire based on features of the area (geometry), volume of gas and so on.

- If the ignition produces an explosion, what will be the explosion pressure? Explosion-simulating models have been developed, which predict pressures and take into account the numerous factors that affect the outcome of such an event.

In such consequence analyses, the models used form an important part of the background knowledge. The probabilities assigned are conditional on the models used.

4.4   Probabilities and uncertainties

The analysis has so far provided a set of event chains (scenarios). However, how likely are these different scenarios and the associated consequences? Some scenarios can be very serious should they occur, but if the probability is low, they are not so critical.

Probabilities and expected values are used to express the risk. However, all types of uncertainties associated with what will be the consequences are not reflected through the probabilities. As discussed in Chapter 2, a risk description based on probabilities alone does not necessarily provide a sufficiently informative picture of the risk. The probabilities are conditional on a certain background knowledge, and in many cases, it is difficult to transform uncertainty to probability figures. For a method to assess the strength of the background knowledge, see Section 2.4.

In a simple consequence analysis, only one consequence value is specified, even though different outcomes are possible. This value is normally interpreted as the expected value should the initiating event occur. If such an approach is used, one must be aware that there is uncertainty about which consequences can occur. This problem is discussed in more detail in Sections 2.3 and 4.5.

Example

A firm installs and services telephone and data cables. There have been a number of events where such cables have been cut due to excavation work, and this has led to several companies being without telephone and internet connection for several days. As a part of a larger risk and vulnerability analysis, the undesirable event 'breakage of buried cable' is studied. A consequence analysis is conducted to describe the possible results of such cable breakages. The analysis concludes that the consequences could range from a few subscribers being without connection to rupture of the entire communication linkage between two large cities. The probability that the most serious incident would occur is calculated to be very low. If the analysis group restricts its attention to the expected consequences – that some companies will be without connection – specifies a probability for this event and carries this information further into the analysis, then an important aspect of the risk picture will not be captured, namely, that it is actually possible to have a complete rupture of the traffic between two large cities.

Reflection

How do we determine the initiating events?

The challenge is to select the initiating events that are such that

- they collectively cover the entire risk picture;

- the number is not too large;

- the consecutive modelling supports the objective of the analysis.

In a processing plant, process leakages are often selected as initiating events. If we had looked further backwards along the causal chains, it would have been difficult to cover all the relevant scenarios, and the number would have increased significantly. If we had looked forward along the consequence chains, for example, to process-related fires, we will be forced to condition on different leakage scenarios, which means that we in fact reintroduce leakages as the initiating events. For fires we have considerably less historical data than leakages; hence, a fire cause analysis is required. And such a cause analysis is preferably carried out by introducing leakage as the initiating event. Alternatively, we may adopt a backwards approach as mentioned in Section 3.2, where leakages that could lead to a specific fire scenario are identified.

We conclude that the analysis is simpler and more structured if we choose to use leakage as the initiating event. However, what is the best choice is of course dependent on the objectives of the analysis.

4.5   Risk picture: risk presentation

The risk picture is established based on the cause analysis and the consequence analysis. The picture covers (A, C, P, K), where A refers to the specified initiating events, C the defined consequences, P the probabilities that express how likely various events and outcomes are and K is the background knowledge on which A, C and P are based. In Chapters 7–13, we provide a number of examples showing this picture in various situations. See also Chapter 2. Generally, the risk picture will cover

- predictions (often expected values) of the quantities we are interested in (e.g. costs, number of fatalities);

- probability distributions, for example, related to costs and number of fatalities;

- strength of knowledge.

- manageability factors.

Depending on the objective and the type of analysis, the risk picture can be limited to some defined areas and issues. Let us look at an example.

Example

Assume that a consequence analysis is carried out for the undesirable event 'shutdown of system S', where system S is an ICT system that is used during surgical interventions at a hospital. Based on experience, it is expected that system S will shut down once every year. Until now, this has not led to serious consequences for

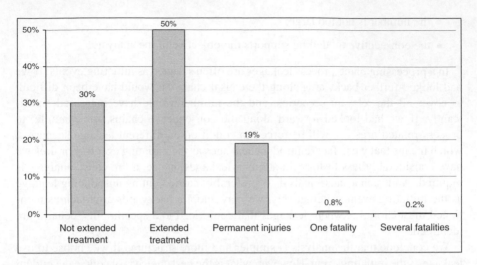

Figure 4.4   Probability of various consequences should the undesirable event occur.

the patients, but the staff at the hospital acknowledge that the consequences could be serious under slightly different circumstances. This is the background for conducting a consequence analysis.

There are uncertainties about the consequences of shutdown of system S. As a simplification, the various outcomes are divided into five categories. The uncertainty about what will happen if system S shuts down is quantified by means of probabilities, as shown in Figure 4.4. We see that these probabilities add up to 100%; hence, if the initiating event occurs, then one of these consequences must take place.

The figure shows that shutdown of system S will most likely bring about extended treatment for some patients, but the event can lead to a spectrum of consequences ranging all the way from insignificant consequences to death of several patients. The initiating (undesirable) event can lead to consequences of varying seriousness, as showns in the figure.

The probabilities indicate how likely it is that the consequence will be 'not extended treatment', 'extended treatment' and so on. If we choose to present the probability – consequence dimensions in a risk matrix, how should we do this? A common method is to present the expected consequence of the event, that is, $E[C|A]$, where we, as mentioned earlier, denote the consequence by C and the event by A. The expected value is, in principle, the centre of gravity in Figure 4.4. However, since the consequence categories are described by text and not numbers, we cannot calculate this centre point mathematically. Furthermore, to compare the extended treatment with number of deaths is to integrate consequences having different dimensions. A 'typical' solution will be to use the consequence 'extended treatment' as the expected value, since this consequence corresponds to an approximate centre in the figure, with 30% of the probability mass on the one side and 20% on the

Probability/ frequency		Consequences				
		Not extended treatment	Extended treatment	Permanent injuries	One fatality	Several fatalities
	Prediction of >10 events over 1 year					
	Prediction of 1–10 events over 1 year	✹	✹ ◭			
	10–50% probability of one event over 1 year			✹		
	1–10% probability of one event over 1 year					
	<1% probability of one event over 1 year				✹	✹

 E[C|A]: Expected consequence if the undesirable event A occurs

 P(C_i|A): Probability/frequency for consequence C_i if the undesirable event A occurs

Figure 4.5   Example of a risk matrix.

other side. The expected consequence of the undesirable event is indicated by the triangular symbol in the risk matrix in Figure 4.5.

From the example, we see that a risk description based on expected values does not give a particularly good picture of the risk. The consequence spectrum is not revealed. However, it is also possible to plot the consequence categories instead of the expected value. We then plot the points from Figure 4.4 directly:

- Not extended treatment: 30% probability

- Extended treatment: 50% probability

- Permanent injury: 19% probability

- One fatality: 0.8% probability

- Several fatalities: 0.2% probability.

These points are plotted in Figure 4.5 by using star-shaped symbols. This method of presenting the risk provides a more nuanced picture, since we show the range of different potential consequences, rather than just the expected consequences.

On the other hand, the volume of information can become too large when one tries to differentiate between all possible consequences. Using just one point makes it easier to compare risk contributions for the different events. The result is that in practice many are using the risk matrix based on $E[C|A]$, even though it can give a misleading picture of the risk.

The difference in the two methods used to plot the risk corresponds to the difference in Figures 2.1 and 2.2. If an event is located high to the right, the risk is high, whereas it is low if placed low to the left. Whether or not the risk is considered too high or acceptable is another issue. One often sees that the risk matrix is subdivided into three areas, upwards to the right indicates unacceptable risk, below to the left is the negligible risk zone and the middle zone is the ALARP area where the risks should be reduced to a level that is as low as reasonably practicable. We do not, however, use such a subdivision in this book, since we are, in principle, sceptical about the use of such pre-defined risk acceptance limits. See the discussion in Section 13.3.3. What is a tolerable risk and an acceptable risk cannot be considered in isolation from other considerations, for example, costs. On the other hand, it could be appropriate to have established standards or reference values that can tell what typically are the high and low values for the risk. In this way, it is much easier to sort out what is important and what is not.

Of importance in this context is the recognition that risk is more than just the numbers in the risk matrix. All probabilities and expected values are characterised by a certain background knowledge K. The probability $P(A)$ should be written $P(A|K)$. The background knowledge is a part of the risk picture and the risk presentation. We return to the issue in Section 4.5.1.

The above example shows the importance of looking at uncertainties beyond the expected values. We have repeatedly pointed out that it is necessary to look beyond the probabilities and expected values in order to view all aspects of uncertainty. The probabilities are not perfect tools for expressing uncertainty. The assumptions can hide important aspects of risk and uncertainty, and our lack of knowledge may lead to probabilities and expectations resulting in poor predictions. We shall see more examples of this in Chapters 7–13.

4.5.1   Handling the background knowledge

The risk description is conditional on the background knowledge K as discussed in Chapter 2. This also applies to risk matrices, such as Figure 4.5. To reflect the strength of the background knowledge, we could perform an assessment as outlined in Section 2.4 and obtain an adjusted risk matrix as shown in Figure 2.6. We may for example show a risk matrix in which all the points in Figure 2.6 are to be understood as having a strong background knowledge except the one for several fatalities where the symbol is dashed to indicate that the background knowledge is considered to be of a medium strength.

Let us consider another example. You are carrying out a risk analysis of an offshore installation. The first part of the analysis is identification of initiating events. During the course of the process, a number of assumptions are made regarding operational conditions, certain risk-reducing measures that are in place, a certain manning level and so on.

Later on, a model-based risk analysis of an initiating event, 'leakage in a gas line into the first-stage separator', is carried out. In this analysis, assumptions are made regarding pressure, temperature, composition, which valves are open/closed, how often valves are tested, how long it would take for valves to close, the level of personnel in the various sections of the platform, emergency preparedness routines and so on. Computer programmes are used to simulate the gas discharge rate and relevant fire and explosion development. The programmes make use of various models, which, in turn, are based on a number of conditions and assumptions. Some of these are built into the model, while others can be controlled by the person conducting the risk analysis.

In other words, many assumptions are made during the course of the analysis process. These assumptions must be documented in a systematic way, and they must be presented to those who use the risk analysis for decision-making. The results obtained from the risk analyses must be viewed in the light of the assumptions made. Operational personnel should be aware of these assumptions, and it is essential that the assumptions are incorporated into the maintenance programme and the emergency preparedness planning and so on. In practice, it is a challenge to achieve all this successfully.

Sensitivity and robustness analyses

The risk picture is not complete unless we have carried out sensitivity and robustness analyses. These analyses show to what extent the results are dependent on important conditions and assumptions, and what it takes for the conclusions to be changed.

The depth of such analyses will, of course, depend on the decision problem, the risks that are analysed and the available resources.

Sensitivity analysis can be carried out on both the causal and consequence sides of initiating events. In the analysis, we study how the calculated risk changes its direction in response to changes in the information that the analysis is based on, for example, the probabilities used in event trees or in fault trees. An example is shown in Figure 4.6. The figure shows the effect on individual risk of increasing the helicopter transport for an offshore oil and gas field.

In practice, we often start with the conclusion and ask what it takes for it to change. One can then 'go backwards' in the analysis and find out which conditions have a significant impact on the conclusion. We are talking about a robustness analysis. Carrying out sensitivity analyses on all conditions is not feasible in practice.

4.5.2   Risk evaluation

The discussion above has covered the key steps of a risk analysis, but it has also touched upon risk evaluation. Consider the discussion in the above example on what

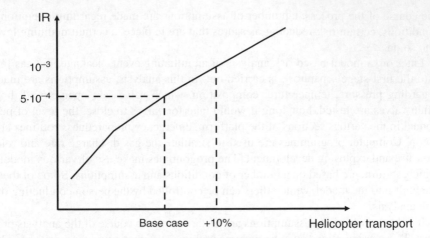

Figure 4.6   Example of sensitivity analysis.

represents tolerable or acceptable risk. The risk evaluation will however be more thoroughly studied in the risk treatment discussion in Chapter 5. Through the risk analysis and the discussion of the results, the analysts will be able to give their message (the risk picture and the risk presentation), and then the management and decision-makers will become more central – we have entered the risk treatment chapter (Chapter 5).

5

The risk analysis process: risk treatment

This chapter looks closer into risk treatment, and the following main steps (refer Figure 1.2):

- comparison of alternatives and identification and assessment of measures (for short referred to as *comparison of alternatives*);

- management review and judgement.

Risk treatment is the process of selection and implementation of measures to modify risk, including measures to avoid, reduce, optimise and transfer risk (refer Section 1.2). How one chooses to treat risk will depend on which type of strategy the organisation has in place for the risk management.

5.1 Comparisons of alternatives

In Section 3.1, we reviewed the most common ways of using the risk analysis in the decision-making process:

- Look at changes in risk

- Cost-effectiveness analysis

- Cost-benefit analysis

- Risk acceptance criteria (tolerability limits)

- ALARP assessment.

Risk Analysis, Second Edition. Terje Aven.
© 2015 John Wiley & Sons, Ltd. Published 2015 by John Wiley & Sons, Ltd.

We compare alternatives by looking at the risk picture for the various alternatives. If the alternatives are about the same with respect to other concerns, such as costs, the risk analysis gives a good basis for recommending a particular alternative. Normally, we must, however, undertake a weighing between various concerns, and then the cost-effectiveness analysis and the cost-benefit analysis come into play. These analyses make it possible to compare the various concerns, such as risk and costs. These analyses do not, however, provide answers to what is the correct solution and the best alternative. As is the case for all types of analyses, these analyses have their limitations and weaknesses, and they can only provide a basis for making a good decision.

The main problem of the cost-benefit analysis is related to the transformation of non-economic consequences to monetary values. What is the value of future generations? How should we determine a 'correct' discount rate? The value of safety and security is not adequately taken into account by the approach. Investments in safety and security are justified by risk and uncertainty reductions, but cost-benefit analyses to a large extent ignore these risks and uncertainties. A cost-benefit analysis calculating the expected net present values does not take into account the risks (uncertainties). To explain this in more detail, consider the following example:

> In an industry, two risk-reducing measures I and II are considered. For measure I (II), the computed expected reduced number of fatalities equals 1 (2). The costs are identical for the two measures. Hence the cost-benefit approach would guide the decision-maker to give priority to measure II. But suppose that there are large uncertainties about the phenomena and processes that could lead to fatalities. Say for example that measure II is based on new technology. Would that change the conclusion of the cost-benefit analysis? No, because this analysis restricts attention to the expected value. We conclude that there is a need for seeing beyond the expected value calculations and the cost-benefit analysis when determining the best alternative.

For a specific alternative, the risk analysis will provide a basis for arriving at measures that can modify the risk. Such measures could be either probability reducing or consequence reducing, depending on whether they apply to the right or to the left side of the bow-tie diagram (Figure 1.1). When measures are to be identified, a natural strategy will be to take as the starting point those systems and events that contribute most to the risk.

Reflection

How should we identify the areas and factors that contribute the most to risk?

One way of doing this is by looking at the change in risk if this area or factor had contributed insignificantly to the risk. If the change is large, then this area or this factor is important. See Section 13.9.

In the planning phase of a system or an activity, alternatives and measures will be generated as an integrated part of the organisation's general management processes. The risk analysis work must be an integral part of these processes, and based on the tasks and functions to be fulfilled, the various disciplines must come up with possible alternatives and measures.

ALARP assessments require that appropriate measures be generated. If the aim is to satisfy the risk acceptance criteria or tolerability limits, there may be little incentive for identifying risk-reducing measures if the criteria and limits are relatively easy to meet. Risk acceptance (tolerability) can in such cases be reached without implementing specific measures.

As a rule, some suggestions for measures always arise in a risk analysis context, but often a systematic approach for the generation of these is lacking. In many cases, the measures also lack ambitions. They bring about only small changes in the risk picture. A possible way to approach this problem is to apply the following principles:

1. On the basis of existing solutions (base case), identify measures that can reduce the risk by, for example, 10%, 50% and 90%.

2. Specify solutions and measures that can contribute to reaching these levels.

The solutions and measures must then be assessed prior to making a decision on possible implementation.

5.1.1   How to assess measures?

Measures that are identified/suggested are analysed using the principles defined in Section 3.1 and further discussed in this chapter. The measures will, in some cases, have exclusively positive effects (e.g. improved safety), but in many instances the measures could produce both positive and negative effects. An example of this is a measure relating to the use of chemicals, which reduces the risk to personnel but which leads to increased risk for negative impact on the external environment. Another example is the installation of new safety systems that seem to be positive in an accident situation, but this installation increases the system complexity and increases the need for maintenance. The method by which the measures are analysed, however, may remain the same, whether the measures have only positive effects or both positive and negative effects.

As pointed out in Section 3.1, it will often be appropriate to undertake crude analyses of the measures as a screening process to identify measures that clearly should be implemented and those that require more detailed analyses.

Conclusions are often self-evident when computing indices such as the expected cost per expected life saved or expected cost per expected reduced ton of oil over the life cycle of a project. For example, a strategy may be that measures will be implemented if the expected cost per expected life saved is < €10 million.

A measure that has positive expected present value should be implemented immediately. Crude computations of the expected present value, where one leaves out difficult assessments related to the value of loss of life and damage to the environment, will often be sufficient for concluding to what extent this criterion can justify the implementation of a measure.

A potential strategy for the assessment of a measure, if the analysis based on expected present value or expected cost per expected number of lives saved has not produced any clear recommendation, can be that the measure be implemented if for several of the following questions the answer is in the affirmative:

- Is there a relatively high personnel risk or environmental risk?

- Is there considerable uncertainty (related to phenomena, consequences and conditions) and will the measure reduce the uncertainties?

- Will the measure significantly increase manageability? High competence among the personnel can give increased assurance that satisfactory outcomes will be reached, for example, fewer leakages.

- Is the measure contributing towards obtaining a more robust solution?

- Is the measure based on Best Available Technology (BAT)?

- Are there unsolved problem areas that are personnel safety-related and/or work environment-related? Are there possible areas where there is conflict between these two aspects?

- Are there strategic considerations?

Reflection

In the assessment of various measures, one often forgets that a measure in many instances also has negative effects, with respect to not only costs but also safety of personnel.

On the gas transport pipeline from Platform A to onshore, there is an underwater valve that should shut off in the event of leakage in the risers or in the topside riser valve. This valve is defined as safety critical, and in accordance with normal practice and regulatory requirements, it must be tested annually.

The testing of the valve is a risk-reducing measure to ensure that the valve functions in the event of an accident. If the valve does not function in the event of large-scale leakages/fires, then this can obstruct personnel from escaping over a bridge to Platform B. They can become trapped on Platform A. In addition, failure of the valve will result in considerable material losses.

At the same time, one realises that the testing of such a valve is a demanding undertaking and leads to a risk for those persons that carry out this work. Experience shows that a large part of the leakages occur during the closing down and the run-up of the facility. In consideration of the safety of the maintenance personnel, the maintenance should not take place more often than is absolutely necessary.

The maintenance activities are also of utmost importance economically, as several platforms must shut down while the testing takes place. There is also a danger that a valve might not open following testing. In the case of an underwater valve such as this, the result could be a production shutdown at several platforms over 1–2 weeks, causing huge economic losses.

How often should we test these valves? All relevant factors should be considered prior to making a decision. In this case, we seek to find a solution whereby maintenance is carried out as seldom as possible, but often enough to ensure that the valve will function with a sufficiently high probability if an accident should occur. However, a simple formula that provides a solution to the problem does not exist.

5.2 Management review and judgement

When various solutions and measures are to be compared and a decision is to be made, the analysis and assessments that have been conducted provide a basis for such a decision. In many cases, established design principles and standards also provide clear guidance. Compliance with such principles and standards will be among the first reference points when assessing risks.

It is common thinking that risk management processes, and especially ALARP processes, require formal guidelines or criteria (e.g. risk acceptance criteria and cost-effectiveness indices) to simplify the decision-making. Care has however to be shown when using this type of formal decision-making criteria, as they easily result in a mechanisation of the decision-making process. Such a mechanisation is unfortunate because of the following:

1. Decision-making criteria based on risk-related numbers (probabilities and expected values) alone do not capture all the aspects of risk, costs and benefits.

2. No method has a precision that justifies a mechanical decision based on whether the result is over or below a numerical criterion.

3. It is a managerial responsibility to make decisions under uncertainty, and management should be aware of the relevant risks and uncertainties.

The reader is referred to the discussion in Chapter 13.

Example of management review and judgement

An oil company has two undersea pipelines supplying an important customer with natural gas. The gas is produced at two different processing facilities and fed into the two pipelines. En route, the pressure drops to a level where it is considerably lower at the delivery end. The delivery takes place at two different sites located at a considerable distance from each other. The company is of the opinion that if it installs a plant for gas pressure boosting (a pumping station) between the processing facility and the delivery site, it will be able to deliver more gas through the pipeline. The company is evaluating various alternative solutions for pressure boosting:

1. Two separate installations – one for each pipeline.

2. A single installation for compressing the gas. This solution means that the single pipeline must be re-routed over several kilometres.

Alternative 2 is significantly less expensive than alternative 1.

The various alternatives are assessed and compared in a risk analysis. The conclusion of the analysis is that the risks for both personnel and the environment are low for the single installation solution.

The management then undertakes a management review and judgement. Today there are no 'probable' events that could simultaneously stop delivery in both pipelines as the processing facilities, pipelines and delivery sites are separate. The company does not wish to increase its vulnerability by setting up a common point for these two independent systems. In the case of an event at the installation proposed in alternative 2, this could have an impact on the entire gas supply to the customer. For this reason, alternative 2 is rejected and alternative 1 is implemented.

Reflection

To verify, ALARP, procedures based on engineering judgements and codes are used, but also traditional cost-benefit analyses and cost-effectiveness indices. When using such analyses, guidance values are often used, to specify values that define 'gross disproportion'. A typical number for a value of statistical life used in cost-benefit analysis is £1–2 million (HSE 2003, Aven and Vinnem 2005). For certain areas the numbers are much higher, for example, in the offshore UK industry it is common to use $6 million (HSE 2006). This increased number is said to account for the potential for multiple fatalities and uncertainty and may be viewed as an extra weight justified by the ALARP principle and the principle of 'reversed burden of proof'. What is your response to this practice?

This practice is indeed questionable, as the expected net present value calculations performed in a cost-benefit analysis do not adequately reflect the risk and uncertainties as discussed in Section 5.1. It can be discussed whether the ALARP principle with its gross disproportion criterion should imply a higher value of a statistical life than normal, but the argument would not be the risk and the uncertainties. Moreover, one may also question why more resources should be used on safety measures for one group than for another. Does this mean that society has a stronger preference for avoiding fatalities in one specific group of people?

6

Risk analysis methods

This chapter presents a selection of methods that can be used when carrying out a risk analysis. These methods are described in detail in the literature and in a number of textbooks within this professional field (Rausand and Høyland 2004, Bedford and Cooke 2001, Vose 2008, to mention a few). In this book, we present a short summary of the most fundamental methods, partly based on Aven (1992).

6.1 Coarse risk analysis

A coarse risk analysis (often also referred to as a *preliminary risk analysis*) is a common method for establishing a crude risk picture, with a relatively modest effort. The analysis covers selected parts of, or the entire, bow-tie (see Figure 1.1), that is, the initiating events, the cause analysis and the consequence analysis. The analysis team typically consists of 3–10 persons.

Often, the coarse risk analysis is performed by dividing the analysis subject into sub-elements and then by carrying out the risk analysis for each of these sub-elements in turn. This applies regardless of whether the analysis focuses on a section of a highway, a production system, an offshore installation or other analysis subjects. Checklists may be used as a tool for identifying and analysing hazards and threats for each sub-element to be analysed.

The form used to document the risk analysis is often standardised. An example of an analysis form for a risk analysis of a road tunnel is shown in Table 6.1. We see from the table that the risk is described by using categories. The categories cover possible undesirable events, along with the probability and expected consequence if such an event should occur. We see from the table that, in the case of a bus fire, we expect that there will be 10 people killed. The number can be 0, 1 or 30, but the expectation is 10.

In stating probabilities, terms such as *often* and *seldom* should be avoided as they are open to different interpretations. A better alternative is to say directly what we

Risk Analysis, Second Edition. Terje Aven.
© 2015 John Wiley & Sons, Ltd. Published 2015 by John Wiley & Sons, Ltd.

Table 6.1   Example of an analysis form for a coarse risk analysis of a road tunnel.

Sub-element	Hazards/causes		Probabilities and consequences		Comments	Risk	Possible measures	Comments
	Undesirable events	Causes	Consequence analysis	Probability analysis				
Between entry points	Traffic accidents	Head-on crash	Turn-around in tunnel because of long queue, smoke, exhaust, etc. Wrong-way entry	1–3 killed	1–10% prob. in 1 year	Can also result in serious injury	High	Signage for wrong-way driving	Measures taken, ongoing assessments, ⋯
Between entry points	Traffic accidents	Rear-end crash	Slow-moving vehicles	Less serious injuries	Several times per year		Low	Detection of slow-moving vehicles	
Passing lane	Traffic accidents	Lane-changing accidents	Breakdown, speed variation, light conditions, road marking	Serious injuries	10–50% prob. in 1 year		Moderate	Detection of slow-moving vehicles	
Entire tunnel	Fire	Bus fire	Technical failure, collision, ignition	10 killed	Below 1% prob. in 1 year	Outcome uncertainties	Moderate	Fire-extinguish. equipment, ventilation	To be assessed in the detailed analysis

mean, for example, 10–50% probability that an event will occur within the period of 1 year. Some people will perhaps say that it is difficult for the analysis group to express that there is a 1–10% probability or a 10–50% probability, for example. The answer to this is 'yes', it can be difficult to assign probabilities. However, it does not help 'hiding' behind expressions such as 'often' or 'seldom' without explaining what one means by these terms. Also, the consequence categories should be precisely defined, rather than using terms such as *high*, *low* and so on.

A coarse risk analysis is often combined with other analysis methods. The coarse analysis identifies the most important risk contributors, and then the causal picture and/or the consequence picture can be assessed in detail using more detailed analyses.

Example: workplace accidents

The working environment committee at the Packing Factory Ltd has found that in the bag department, which has about 90 employees, the number of injuries is too high. The committee therefore decides to implement some injury preventive measures to reduce the injury rate in the department. It is, however, not clear where such measures should be directed and which measures would most effectively prevent injuries. Opinions in the working environment committee differ widely.

In the bag department, production is a series production of large, multiple ply paper bags. Each production line comprises several machines. The raw material is paper rolls. The main operator task in the department is to monitor and adjust the machines. Some operators deal with manual handling of products. It is the operators who are operating the machines that are most exposed to injuries.

The working environment committee instructs the safety delegate of the company to work out a basis for decisions on preventing measures. The safety delegate is familiar with risk analyses and uses such an analysis to establish the desired decision basis.

By means of the risk analysis, the safety delegate will identify possible injuries that might occur in the department, where they might occur, possible causes and the severity of the injuries. Table 6.2 presents a summary of the analysed hazards. With respect to probability/frequency, the following classification is used:

1. Very unlikely: less than once per 1000 years (yearly probability 1:1000)

2. Unlikely: once per 100 years (yearly probability 1:100)

3. Quite likely: once per 10 years (yearly probability 1:10)

4. Likely: once per year

5. Frequently: once per month or more frequently.

Also for the consequences five categories are used:

 I. Does not result in injuries

 II. Minor injuries

Table 6.2 Summary of identified hazards.

No	Event	Cause	Consequence	Probability	Consequence category
1.	Crushing in cutting machinery	Hand in running machine, e.g., due to inattention	Finger/hand injury	4	III
2.	Crushing in pulling machinery	As in 1	Finger/hand injury	4	III
3.	Crushing at intermediate station	As in 1	Finger/hand injury	3	III
4.	Damage at guillotine	As in 1	Finger/hand injury	3	III
5.	Being caught at the glue station	Inattention	Hand/arm injury	3	III
6.	Being caught in folding station	Missing cover inattention	Significant body injuries	3	IV
7.	Crushing between rollers	As 1	Finger/hand injury	4	III
8.	Damage from machinery splinter	Rupture during operation	Major wounds	4	II
9.	Knocks from edge, machine part, etc.	Inattention	Wounds, cuts	4	I
10.	Hair or clothes being caught between rollers	Inattention	Significant body injuries	2	IV
11.	Bodily damage from unobserved machinery start-up	Technical failure, noise, inattention	Significant body injuries	2	IV
12.	Crushing when lifting roll	Inattention	Finger/hand injuries	4	III
13.	Damage due to roll coming loose	Rupture of spindle, carelessness	Severe injuries, fatalities	2	V
14.	Damage due to dropping roll	Failure of tackle, inadequate fastening	Severe injuries, fatalities	4	V
15.	Paper fire	Ignition of paper dust oil, weld sparks, smoking	Loss of casings/sacks, destruction of machines	3	I

Consequence category

Probability category	I	II	III	IV	V
1					
2				10, –11	13
3	15		3, 4, 5	6	
4	9	8	1, 2, 7, 12		14
5					

Figure 6.1   Probability (frequency)–consequence diagram.

III. Major injuries

IV. Death or total disability

V. Death or total disability for several persons.

The starting point for the hazard identification was the injury reports for the whole department for the last 9 years. Data on near misses were also available. In addition, the system description was studied to identify other hazards. For the hazards based on the injury reports, the classification is based on this statistics. For example, two injuries caused by crushing in the cutting machinery are registered. This gives a classification 'likely'. Judgement has been used for the hazards that are not based on the injury statistics.

In Figure 6.1, the hazards have been placed in a consequence probability diagram. The consequence categories are marked along the horizontal axis with consequences increasing to the right. Similarly, frequency/probability is marked along the vertical axis, with frequency increasing downwards. The following conclusions are drawn:

- Highest risk: hazard number 14, which equals 'paper roll falls from tackle'

- Other contributors to high risk are: events that include crushing and catching in the machinery.

The events with the lowest risk are numbers 9 and 15. Thus, in general, for this type of consequence probability diagram, the events with the highest risk are those in the bottom right corner, whereas the events with the lowest risk are placed in the upper left corner. We should, however, be very careful when drawing conclusions from the matrix since it is based on a rough classification and is based a probability–consequence description only, not for example expressing the strength of knowledge on which the assignments are based.

Note that hazard 15 (paper fire) has low risk in relation to personnel. If we focus on material assets or economic values, this hazard would contribute much more to risk.

Based on the risk analysis, the safety delegate can now identify and rank measures to prevent accidents, as a basis for the decision-making on which measures to implement.

6.2   Job safety analysis

A job safety analysis is a simple qualitative risk analysis methodology used to identify the hazards that are associated with a work assignment that is to be executed. A job safety analysis is usually checklist-based. Normally, the persons planning/executing the work assignment are part of the analysis team. By carrying out a job safety analysis, we ensure the following:

- It is clarified whether the work assignment is a 'standard' operation that can be carried out according to procedures and normal practice or whether it is a non-standard case that requires special measures or studies. The latter case may lead to postponement until more detailed studies are carried out.

- Possible conflicts between different jobs may be identified; for example, painting and welding jobs close to each other at the same time.

- The persons carrying out the work assignment will think through what they should do and consider each work assignment in a risk-related perspective. The mere act of thinking through and planning the work assignments can, in itself, be a risk-reducing measure.

- What can go wrong at the various steps of the job will be assessed. Through this process, those carrying out the job will become aware of the most risky aspects of the work assignment, and adequate risk-reducing measures can then be implemented.

A job safety analysis is carried out by dividing the job into a number of sub-jobs or tasks and then performing an analysis for each task. The division into tasks is illustrated by the following example:

Change of a car wheel
  1. Set the hand brake.

  2. Take out the spare wheel from the boot.

  3. Check the air pressure.

  4. Remove the hub cap.

  5. Ensure that the jack fits and is stable.

6. Jack up the car, but not so much that the wheels leave the ground.

7. Loosen the wheel nuts.

8. Jack up the car further, but not more than is necessary.

9. Remove the wheel and so on.

The identification of hazards includes a check of the following:

- What type of injuries that may occur, for example, crushing?

- Are special problems or deviations likely to occur?

- Is the task difficult or uncomfortable to carry out?

- Are there alternative ways of carrying out the task?

The identified hazards are assessed and the conclusions categorised, for example, in the following way:

0 insignificant risk

1 acceptable risk; actions unnecessary

2 the risk should be reduced

3 the risk must be reduced; there is a need for immediate actions.

When evaluating the risk and the need for actions/risk-reducing measures, considerations should be given to, for example:

- violation of statutory requirements;

- violation of requirements set by the company;

- high risk documented by means of accident statistics;

- high energy concentration;

- unreasonable requirements with respect to attention and vigilance for the operator;

- low tolerance for human errors in the technical system;

- whether the solution of the problem is known and available.

Special sheets have been developed for job safety analysis. Such sheets will typically include the following main points:

- Description of the job

- Accident experience (statistics)

- Accident potential

- Requirements
- Job sequence (tasks)
- Risk assessment
- Actions/measures.

Often, the sheets include a list of possible actions that are to be considered. The actions may, for example, be related to improved equipment and tools, better work instructions, improved education and training and so on.

6.3   Failure modes and effects analysis

Failure Modes and Effects Analysis (FMEA) is an analysis method to reveal possible failures and to predict the failure effects on the system as a whole. The method is inductive; for each component of the system, we investigate what happens if this component fails. The method represents a systematic analysis of the components of the system to identify all significant failure modes and to see how important they are for the system's performance. Only one component is considered a time, and the other components are then assumed to function perfectly. FMEA is therefore not suitable for revealing critical combinations of component failures.

FMEA was developed in the 1950s and was one of the first systematic methods used to analyse failures in technical systems. The method has appeared with different names and with somewhat different content. If we describe or rank the criticality of the various failures in the FMEA, the analysis is often referred to as an FMECA (Failure Modes, Effects and Criticality Analysis). The criticality is a function of the failure effect and the frequency/probability as seen below. The difference between an FMEA and an FMECA is not distinct, and in this book, we do not distinguish between these two methods. In the following, we also use the term *FMEA* when the analysis includes a description/ranking of criticality.

In several enterprises, it is nowadays a requirement that an FMEA be included as part of the design process and that the results from the analysis be part of the system documentation.

To ensure a systematic study of the system, a specific FMEA form is used. The FMEA form may, for example, include the following columns:

Identification (column 1). Here the specific component is identified by a description and/or number. It is also common to refer to a system drawing or a functional diagram.

Function, operational state (column 2). The function of the component, that is, its working tasks in the system, is briefly described.

    The state of the component when the system is in normal operation, is described, for example, whether it is in a continuous operation mode or in a stand-by mode.

Failure modes (column 3). All the possible ways the components can fail to perform its function are listed in this column. Only the failure modes that can be observed from 'outside' are included. The internal failure modes are to be considered as failure causes. These causes can possibly be listed in a separate column. In some cases, it will also be of interest to look at the basic physical and chemical processes that can lead to failure (failure mechanisms), such as corrosion.

Often we also state how the different failure modes of the component are detected and by whom.

Example: In a chemical process plant, a specific valve is considered as a component in the system. The function of the valve is to open and close on demand. 'The valve does not open on a demand' and 'the valve does not close on a demand' are relevant failure modes, as well as 'the valve opens when not intended' and 'the valve closes when not intended'. However, 'washer bursts' is an example of a cause of a specific failure mode.

Effect on other units in the system (column 4). In those cases where the specific failure mode affects other components in the system, this is stated in this column. Emphasis should be given to identification of failure propagation, which does not follow the functional chains of the functional diagrams. For example, increased load on the remaining pillars that are supporting a common load when a pillar collapses; vibration in a pumping house may induce failure of the driving unit of the pump and so on.

Effect on system (column 5). In this column, we describe how the system is influenced by a specific failure mode. The operational state of the system as a result of failure is to be expressed, for example, whether the system is in the operational state, changed to another operational mode or not in an operational state.

Corrective measures (column 6). Here, we describe what has been done or what can be done to correct the failure, or possibly to reduce the consequences of the failure. We may also list the measures that are aimed at reducing the probability that failure will occur.

Failure frequency (column 7). In this column, we state the assigned frequency (probability) for a specific failure mode and consequence. Instead of presenting frequencies for all the different failure modes, we may give a total frequency and relative frequencies (in percentages) for the different failure modes.

Failure effect ranking (column 8). A failure is ranked according to its effect with respect to reliability and safety, possibilities of mitigating the failure, length of the repair time, production loss and so on. We might, for example, use the following grouping of failure effects:

Small: A failure that does not reduce the functional ability of the system more than normally is accepted.

Large: A failure that reduces the functional ability of the system beyond the acceptable level, but the consequences can be corrected and controlled.

Critical: A failure that reduces the functional ability of the system beyond the acceptable level and that creates an unacceptable condition, either operational or with respect to safety.

Remarks (column 9). Here we state, for example, assumptions and suppositions. By combining the failure frequency (probability) and the failure effect (consequence), the criticality of a specific failure mode is determined.

Example: storage tank

Figure 6.2 shows a tank that functions as a buffer storage for the transport of fluid from the source to the consumer. The consumption of fluid is not constant, and the liquid level will therefore vary. The control of avoiding overfilling of the buffer storage is automatic and can be described as follows: when the liquid level reaches a certain height – 'normal high', then the Level Switch High (LSH) will be activated and LSHH sends a closure signal to valve V1. The fluid supply to the tank then stops. If this mechanism does not function, and the liquid level continues to increase to 'abnormally high level', then the Level Switch High High (LSHH) will be activated and LSHH sends a closure signal to valve V2. The fluid supply to tank then stops. At the same time, the LSHH sends an opening signal to valve V3 so that the fluid is drained. The draining pipe has higher capacity than that of the supply pipe.

A simple FMEA has been carried out for this system. Tables 6.3 and 6.4 show the completed forms for the components LSH, LSHH, V1, V2 and V3. The following ranking of the failure effects is used:

1. There is no fluid supply.

2. The fluid in the tank is drained.

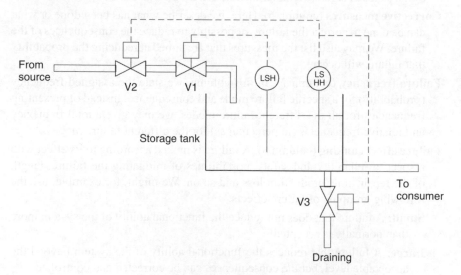

Figure 6.2   Storage tank example.

Table 6.3   Completed FMEA form for storage tank example components LSH, LSHH and V1.

SYSTEM/EQUIPMENT: Storage tank			EXECUTED BY: TAV			PAGE: 1		OF: 2
REF.DIAGRAM/DRAWING.NO.:			DATE: 01.01.08					
Identification	Function/ operational state	Failure mode	Effect on other units in the system	Effect on the system	Corrective measures	Failure frequency	Failure effect ranking	Remarks
1	2	3	4	5	6	7	8	9
LSH	Switch that sends stop signal to V1 if the liquid level is high	Does not send signal when the liquid level is high	V1 does not close	The liquid level may increase abnormally		1% of total number of demands	3	
		Sends signal when the liquid level is not high	V1 closes when not intended	The fluid supply stops		Once per year on average	1	
LSHH	Switch that sends stop signal to V2 and open signal to V3 if the liquid level is abnormally high	Does not send signal when the liquid level is abnormally high	V2 does not close. V3 does not open	The tank is overfilled if V1 does not close		1% of total number of demands	4	
		Sends signal when the liquid level is not abnormally high	V2 closes when not intended, V3 opens when not intended	The tank is drained		Once every second year on average	2	

(continued overleaf)

Table 6.3   (continued)

SYSTEM/EQUIPMENT: Storage tank REF.DIAGRAM/DRAWING.NO.:		EXECUTED BY: TAV DATE: 01.01.08				PAGE: 1	OF: 2	
Identification	Function/ operational state	Failure mode	Effect on other units in the system	Effect on the system	Corrective measures	Failure frequency	Failure effect ranking	Remarks
1	2	3	4	5	6	7	8	9
V1	Stop the fluid supply when the liquid level is high. The valve is normally open	Does not close on signal		The liquid level may increase abnormally		2% of total number of demands	3	
		Close when not intended		The fluid supply stops		Once in 10 years on average	1	
		Significant leakage		The fluid supply stops		Once in 10 years on average	1	

Table 6.4   Completed FMEA form for storage tank example components V2 and V3.

SYSTEM/EQUIPMENT: Storage tank REF.DIAGRAM/DRAWING.NO.:			EXECUTED BY: TAV DATE: 01.01.08			PAGE: 2	OF: 2	
Identification	Function/ operational state	Failure mode	Effect on other units in the system	Effect on the system	Corrective measures	Failure frequency	Failure effect ranking	Remarks
1	2	3	4	5	6	7	8	9
V2	Stop the supply when the liquid level is abnormally high. The valve is normally open	Does not close on signal		Undesired supply to the tank. The fluid is drained if V3 opens		2% of total number of demands	2	
		Closes when not intended		The fluid supply stops		Once in 10 years on average	1	
		Significant leakage		The fluid supply stops		Once in 10 years on average	1	
V3	Drain the fluid when the liquid level is abnormally high. The valve is normally closed	Does not open on signal		Undesired supply to the tank		2% of total number of demands	2	
		Opens when not intended		The fluid is drained		Once in 10 years on average	2	
		Significant leakage		The fluid supply stops. The fluid is drained		Once in 10 years on average	1, 2	

3. The liquid level may increase to an abnormal height.

4. The tank is overfilled if valve V1 does not close.

The consequence categories are crude. For example, there is no indication of the length of a stop in the fluid supply. Only failure modes related to the *normal* operational state have been included. For example, the failure mode 'does not open' is not included for valves V1 and V2.

Now, what are the results of the analysis? First, the analysis of the relevant components has given a good understanding of the type of component failures that might occur and their effects. The analysis demonstrates that the system has a high reliability. The probability that tank is overfilled is small. The component LSHH seems to be the most critical component in the system. We return to the criticality issue in Section 6.6.

6.3.1   Strengths and weaknesses of an FMEA

The strong points of the FMEA are that it gives a systematic overview of the important failures in the system and it forces the designer to evaluate the reliability of his/her system. In addition, it represents a good basis for more comprehensive quantitative analyses, such as fault tree analyses and event tree analyses. Of course, an FMEA gives no guarantee that all critical component failures have been revealed. Through a systematic review such as FMEA, most weaknesses of the system as a result of individual component failures will, however, be revealed.

In an FMEA, the attention is, in many cases, mostly on technical failures, whereas human failure contributions are often overlooked. This may, to some extent, be compensated by including the human functions as components in the system.

An FMEA can be unsuitable for analysing systems with much redundancy (several components that can perform the same function such that failure of one unit does not result in system failure). In such systems, it will not be so interesting to analyse individual component failures, since these cannot directly affect the function of the system. The interest is then focused on combinations of two or more events that together can cause system failure. The storage tank example shows, however, that an FMEA can give valuable information about the possible failures and their effects also for a system with some redundancy. The storage tank system is redundant in that to avoid overfilling of the tank, it is sufficient that valve 1 closes, or that valve 2 closes or valve 3 opens. The analysis is a good starting point for a fault tree analysis or an event tree analysis.

Perhaps the main disadvantage of using the FMEA method is that all components are analysed and documented, also the failures of little or no consequences. An FMEA can therefore be very demanding. The amount of documentation can be extensive. This problem can be reduced by proper component definitions. For the storage tank system, we could have defined the system components by the different parts of valves V1, V2 and V3, and the level switches LSH and LSHH. This would, however, have increased the extent of the analysis considerably, without obtaining more insights into possible undesirable events at the system level. For larger systems, it may be an advantage to define subsystems (system functions). An initial FMEA may be related to failures of these subsystems. Detailed FMEA studies can then be carried out for specific subsystems.

The standard FMEA does not address the strength of knowledge as discussed in Section 2.4, but the method (and the methods considered in the following sections) can easily be adjusted to also cover this aspect.

6.4   Hazard and operability studies

Hazard and Operability (HAZOP) studies is a qualitative risk analysis technique that is used to identify weaknesses and hazards in a processing facility; it is normally used in the planning phase (design). The HAZOP technique was originally developed for chemical processing facilities, but it can also be used for other facilities and systems. For example, it is widely used in Norway in the oil and gas industry.

A HAZOP study is a systematic analysis of how deviation from the design specifications in a system can arise and an analysis of the risk potential of these deviations. Based on a set of *guidewords*, scenarios that may result in a hazard or an operational problem are identified. The following guidewords are commonly used: NO/NOT, MORE OF/LESS OF, AS WELL AS, PART OF, REVERSE and OTHER THAN. The guidewords are related to process conditions, activities, materials, time and place. For example, when analysing a pipe from one unit to another in a process plant, we define the deviation 'no throughput' based on the guideword NO/NOT and the deviation 'higher pressure than the design pressure' based on the guideword MORE OF. Then causes and consequences of the deviation are studied. This is done by asking questions. For example, for the first-mentioned deviation in the pipe example above, the following questions would be asked:

- What must happen to ensure the occurrence of the deviation 'no throughput' (cause)?

- Is such an event possible (relevance/probability)?

- What are the consequences of no throughput (consequence)?

As a support in the work of formulating meaningful questions based on the guidewords, special forms have been developed.

The principle that is used in a HAZOP study can be illustrated in the following way:

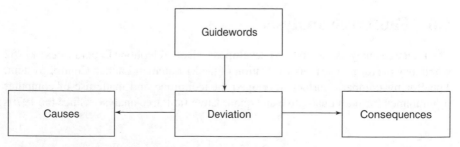

In a HAZOP study, worksheets are used to document deviations, causes, consequences and recommendations/decisions. These worksheets are to be considered as a type of FMEA forms.

A HAZOP study is undertaken by a group of personnel led by a HAZOP leader. The leader should be experienced in using the technique, but does not necessarily need to have thorough knowledge about the actual process. The group comprises persons who have detailed knowledge about the system to be analysed. Typically, the group will consist of five to six persons, in addition to the HAZOP leader.

Through a HAZOP study, critical aspects of the design can be identified, which requires further analysis. Detailed, quantitative reliability and risk analyses will often be generated in this way.

A HAZOP study of a planned plant will, in the same way as an FMEA, normally be most useful if the analysis is undertaken after the Process and Instrumentation Diagrams (PI&Ds) have been worked out. It is at this point in time that sufficient information about the way the plant is to be operated is available.

A HAZOP study is a time- and resource-demanding method. Nevertheless, the method has been widely used in connection with the review of the design of process plants for a safer, more effective and reliable plant.

6.5 SWIFT

Structured What-If Technique (SWIFT) is a risk analysis method in which one uses the lead question – What if – systematically in order to identify deviations from normal conditions. The method is similar to HAZOP in the sense that it utilises a pre-defined checklist of the elements that are to be reviewed. SWIFT is, however, somewhat more flexible than HAZOP, and the checklist can be easily adapted to the application. In a SWIFT analysis, the checklist is reviewed, and we ask, 'what if · · ·' the individual elements on the checklist should occur. In this way, hazardous situations, accident events and so on can be identified. An example of a checklist is shown in Table 6.5.

The analysis is carried out in a manner similar to that used in HAZOP by an analysis team that typically has a variety of competencies, for example, in design, operations, maintenance, safety and so on. In the analysis, possible problems and combinations of conditions that can be problematic are described, and possible risk-reducing measures are identified.

6.6 Fault tree analysis

The fault tree analysis method was developed by Bell Telephone Laboratories in 1962 when they performed a safety evaluation of the Minuteman Launch Control System. The Boeing company further developed the technique and made use of computer programmes for both qualitative and quantitative fault tree analysis. Since the 1970s

Table 6.5   Example of a checklist for use in SWIFT analyses.

Question categories	Examples
Material problems	Flammability, reactivity, toxicity and so on
External effects/impacts	Natural effects (e.g. wind)
	Human-made effects (e.g. falling loads)
Operational failures/human errors	Information, time/sequence, organisation and so on
Supervisory errors/measurement errors	Testing, measurement, management and so on
Equipment/instrument failures	Pumps, valves, computers, power supply and so on
Wrong set-up	Omissions, concurrent operations and so on
Auxiliary system failures	Cooling, fire-fighting water supply, ventilation, communication and so on
Loss of integrity/capacity	Wear and tear, maintenance, overload and so on
Emergency operations	Fire, explosion, toxic spills and so on

fault tree analysis has become widespread and is today one of the most used reliability and risk analysis methods. Its applications are found in most industries. The space industry and the nuclear power industry have perhaps been the two industries that have used fault tree analysis the most.

A fault tree is a logical diagram that shows the relation between system failure, that is, a specific undesirable event, for example, the initiating event of the bow-tie or the failure of a system barrier, and failures of the components of the system. The undesirable event constitutes the *top event* of the tree and the different component failures constitute the *basic events* of the tree. For example, for a production process, the top event might be that the process stops, and one basic event might be that a particular motor fails. A basic event does not necessarily represent a pure component failure; it may also represent human errors or failures that are due to external loads, such as extreme environmental conditions. A fault tree comprises symbols that show the basic events of a system, and the relation between these events and the state of the system. The graphical symbols that show the relation are called *logical gates*. The output from a logical gate is determined by the input states. The graphical symbols vary somewhat depending on the standard that is used. Figure 6.3 shows the most important symbols in a fault tree together with the interpretations of the symbols.

A fault tree that comprises only AND and OR gates can alternatively be represented by a reliability block diagram. This is a logical diagram showing the functional ability of a system. Each component in the system is illustrated by a rectangle as shown in Figure 6.4.

If there is connection from a to b in Figure 6.4, this means that the component is functioning based on the criteria that apply for the particular analysis. Usually,

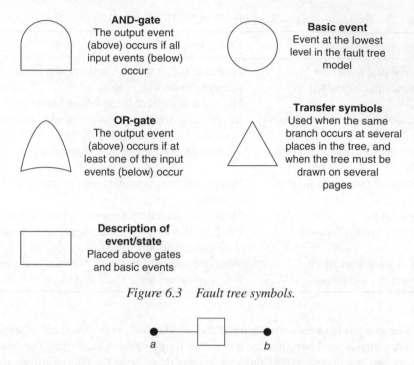

Figure 6.3   Fault tree symbols.

Figure 6.4   Functional element in a reliability block diagram.

'functioning' means absence from one or more failure modes. A presentation of some equivalent fault trees and reliability block diagrams is shown in Figure 6.5.

The top event is the starting point when constructing the fault tree. Next, we must identify the possible failures (events) that can be the direct causes of the top event. These events are linked to the top event by a logical gate. Then, we work successively down to the basic events on the component level. The analysis is deductive and is carried out by repeatedly asking: 'How can this happen?' or 'What are the causes of this event?' The development of the causal sequence is stopped when we have reached the desired level of the detail. It is essential to 'think locally' and to develop the fault tree by using a step-by-step approach. Avoid gate-to-gate connections, that is, connecting one gate directly to the next without providing an intermediate event in between. A common mistake in fault tree construction is over-rapid development of one branch of a tree without proceeding down level by level systematically (tendency to want to reach the basic events too rapidly and not to use broad sub-event descriptions).

Example: tank storage

We consider the tank system described in Section 6.3. The task now is to construct a fault tree for the system with the top event 'overfilling of the tank' and basic events corresponding to failures of the components V1, V2, V3, LSH and LSHH. Figure 6.6

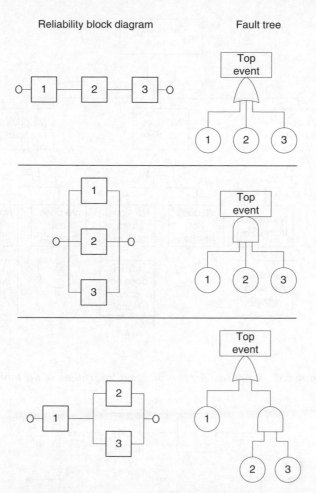

Figure 6.5   Correspondence between reliability block diagrams and fault trees.

shows a fault tree for this top event, with an associated reliability block diagram (Figure 6.7). Note that we disregard the possibility of failure of the transfer of signals from LSH to V1 and from LSHH to V2 and V3.

6.6.1   Qualitative analysis

A fault tree gives valuable information about which failure combinations that can result in an undesirable event. Such a failure combination is called a *cut set*:

A cut set in a fault tree is a set of basic events the occurrence of which ensure that the top event occurs. A cut set is minimal if it cannot be reduced and still ensures the occurrence of the top event.

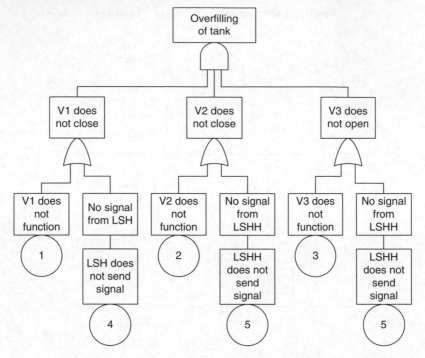

Figure 6.6   Fault tree for the top event 'overfilling of the tank'.

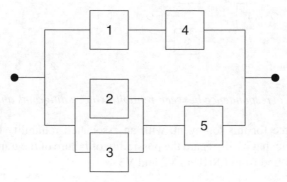

Figure 6.7   Reliability block diagram for the fault tree in Figure 6.6.

For the corresponding reliability block diagram, this definition is equivalent to:

A cut set is a combination of components the failures of which ensure that the system fails. A cut set is minimal if it cannot be reduced without losing its status as a cut set.

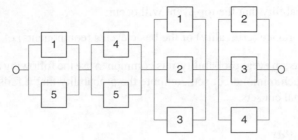

Figure 6.8   The minimal cut set representation of the system in Figure 6.7.

For simple fault trees, the minimal cut sets can be determined directly from the fault tree or from the associated reliability block diagram. In most cases, it would be most convenient to use the reliability block diagram. For more complex fault trees, there is a need for an algorithm. The most known computer-based algorithm is MOCUS (Rausand and Høyland 2004).

Example (cont'd)

The minimal cut sets for the tree in Figure 6.6 are determined directly from the fault tree or its associated reliability diagram:

$$\{1,5\}, \{4,5\}, \{1,2,3\}, \{2,3,4\}.$$

A qualitative analysis of the fault tree is based on an identification of the minimal cut sets. Since system failure occurs when all the events in at least one minimal cut sets occur, the system can be viewed as a series structure of the minimal cut-parallel structures, as shown in Figure 6.8.

The number of events in a cut set is called the *order of the cut set*. The minimal cut sets are ranked according to their order. It may be argued that single-event cut sets (single jeopardy) are highly undesirable as only one failure can lead to the top event, two-event cut sets (double jeopardy) are better and so on. Further ranking based on human errors and active/passive equipment failure is also common. The qualitative approach is however potentially misleading. It may be that larger cut sets have a higher failure probability than smaller ones; this requires a quantitative analysis. Common-cause failures are due to a single event affecting multiple events in the fault tree. This might be a power failure miscalibrating all sensors. Less obviously, elements such as common manufacturer, common location and so on may also lead to common-cause failures.

6.6.2   Quantitative analysis

If we can determine probabilities for the basic events of the fault tree, then we can perform a quantitative analysis. Usually, we would like to calculate

- the probability that the top event will occur;

- the importance (criticality) of the basic events (components) of the tree.

To compute the top event probability, it is common to use the following approximation method: for each minimal cut set, compute the probability that it fails and then sum over all minimal cut sets.

Example (cont'd)

Again we look at the tank example, see the fault tree in Figure 6.6. Assume that the probabilities of the basic events $1, 2, \cdots, 5$ are as given in the FMEA, that is, 2%, 2%, 2%, 1% and 1%. Then using the representation in Figure 6.8, we find that the probability that the top event 'overfilling of the tank' will occur is approximately equal to

$$0.02 \cdot 0.01 + 0.01 \cdot 0.01 + 0.02 \cdot 0.02 \cdot 0.02 + 0.01 \cdot 0.02 \cdot 0.02$$

$$= 0.03 \cdot 10^{-2} = 0.03\%.$$

This means that if the liquid level increases and reaches a high level about 25 times a year, then the probability of overfilling of the tank during a 1-year period would be approximately 0.75% ($= 25 \cdot 0.03\%$). The percentage 0.75 can be viewed as a risk index for the activity. We are allowed to sum the unreliabilities for the 25 cases because the probability that the top event will occur two or more times during 1 year is negligible compared to 0.75%.

We see from these calculations of the probability of the top event that the component 5 (LSHH) is the most important component from a reliability point of view, in the sense that the probability of the top event would be reduced the most by an improvement in the reliability of this component.

The approximation produces accurate results if the probability of the top event is small and the basic events are independent. The basic events are independent if the probability that a basic event will occur does not depend on whether one or more of the other basic events have occurred. Using this approximation method, we disregard the possibility that two or more minimal cut sets will be in the failure state at the same time. For this particular example, the error term is negligible. Alternatively, we can carry out an exact computation, using the fact that the system is a combination of series and parallel structures. The calculations go like this (refer to Appendix B). The components are judged independent. Let p_i be the probability that component i functions as required, $i = 1, 2, \ldots, 5$ and let $q_i = 1 - p_i$. We refer to p_i and q_i as the reliability and unreliability of component i, respectively. Components 1 and 4 are in series; hence, the reliability of this substructure is $p_1 p_4$. Components 2 and 3 are in parallel, and, hence, the unreliability of this substructure is $q_2 q_3$. Combining this substructure and component 5 gives a series structure having reliability $(1 - q_2 q_3) p_5$.

This structure is again in parallel with the structure of components 1 and 4, and we find that the unreliability of the system is equal to

$$(1 - p_1 p_4)[1 - (1 - q_2 q_3) p_5].$$

This exact formula gives an unreliability of 0.03% as above.

Some final remarks concerning the fault tree analysis: the fault tree is easy to understand for persons with no prior knowledge about the technique. The fault tree analysis is well documented and simple to use. One of the advantages of using the technique is that the persons undertaking the analysis is forced to understand the system. Many weak points in the system are revealed and corrected already in the construction phase of the tree. The fault tree analysis gives a static 'picture' of the failure combinations that can cause the top event to occur. The fault tree analysis method is not suitable for analysing systems with dynamic properties. Another problem is treatment of common-mode failures.

There exist many other methods for cause analysis. We would like to mention the *cause-and-effect analysis* (also called *Ishikawa diagram*), which has some similarities to the fault tree analysis but is less structured and does not have the same two-state restriction as a fault tree (Rausand and Høyland 2004). The cause-and-effect analysis is not suited for quantitative analyses.

6.7   Event tree analysis

An event tree analysis is used to study the consequences of the initiating event of a bow-tie diagram. What type of event sequences (scenarios) can the initiating event produce? The method may be used both qualitatively and quantitatively. In the former case, the method provides a picture of the possible scenarios. In the latter case, probabilities are linked to the various event sequences and their consequences.

An event tree analysis is carried out by posing a number of questions where the answer is either 'yes' or 'no'. See the simple example in Figure 6.9. We may interpret the tree as follows: a gas leakage A may occur, and depending on the events B (ignition) and C (escalation), the outcome becomes Y_0, Y_1 or Y_2, where Y represents the number of fatalities or costs (or both). The number of gas leakages in a time interval is denoted X. If an initiating event A occurs, it leads to Y_2 fatalities if both the events B and C occur, Y_1 if the event B occurs and the event C does not occur, and Y_0 if the event B does not occur. Here, Y_2 is equal to zero if B and C do not occur and so on.

From the tree branches, a set of scenarios are generated, as shown by the aforementioned example. It is common to pose the branch questions in such a way that the 'desired' answer is either up (yes) or down (no) for all the branch questions. In this way, the 'best' scenario will come out at one end and the worst scenario, at the other end. If we have many branch questions, we will end up with a large number of event sequences. Often, many of these are almost identical, and it is common to group the various event sequences prior to processing them further in the risk analysis.

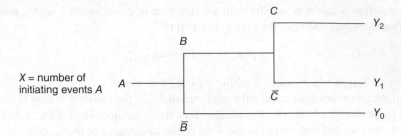

Figure 6.9   Event tree example. Here $\overline{B}$ means 'not B' and so on.

The branch questions can be divided into two main categories:

1. Those related to physical phenomena such as explosions and fires

2. Those related to barriers in the system, such as a fire-fighting system.

Often, the event tree analysis covers both categories. If we wish to reflect the use of various risk-reducing measures, category 2 should be highlighted.

The next step in the analysis will be to draw up a so-called consequence matrix, which describes the consequences arising from each terminating event or group of terminating events. In Figure 6.9, the consequences are restricted to the number of fatalities (Y) and/or costs. The matrix is generated by considering categories of losses. For fatalities we use categories 0, 1 and 2, and for costs categories $<1, 1 - 10, 10 - 100, >100$, say. The maximum number of fatalities is two in this case.

For each scenario s, we need to specify the consequences. This can either be done by using a fixed number, say 2, or expected values, for example, the expected number of fatalities ($E[Y_2|s] = 1.5$ say), or alternatively by determining a probability distribution for the possible outcome categories, for example, $P(Y_2 = 0|s) = 0.10$, $P(Y_2 = 1|s) = 0.30$ and $P(Y_2 = 2|s) = 0.60$.

If probabilities are assigned for branch questions, then a probability can be determined for each terminating event (scenario) by multiplying the probabilities for events in the chain. Let us look at the example of Figure 6.9. Here,

$$P(Y_2 = 2|A) = P(B|A) \cdot P(C|A, B) \cdot P(Y_2 = 2|A, B, C)$$

and unconditionally

$$P(Y_2 = 2) = P(Y_2 = 2|A) \cdot P(A).$$

We have assumed that $P(A)$ is small so that we can ignore the probability of two or more A events during the time interval considered. In the case of more frequent A events, we can use the formula

$$EY = E[Y|A] \cdot EX.$$

It is important to be aware that all the probabilities are conditioned on the earlier events in the event sequence. The probability of two fatalities is not the same in scenario $A - B - C$ as in scenario $A - B - \overline{C}$.

To simplify the analysis, it is common to assume that the outcome is fixed for a specific scenario, and in the following, we assume that $Y_2 = 2$, $Y_1 = 1$ and $Y_0 = 0$. Whether this new model is sufficiently accurate has to be evaluated of course.

Suppose that we arrive at a probability $P(B) = 0.002$, either using modelling or a direct argument using experience data and knowledge about the phenomena and system in question.

Similarly, we determine a probability $P(C|B)$. Let us suppose that we arrive at $P(C|B) = 0.2$. Then, we can calculate the probability distribution for the number of fatalities Y. Approximation formulae such as

$$P(Y = 2) = EX \cdot P(B) \cdot P(C|B), \tag{6.1}$$

are used, which are utilising the probability that the event two or more ignited leakages in 1 year has a negligible probability compared to that of one ignited leakage. Suppose that $EX = 4$. We then obtain $P(Y = 2) = 0.0016$ and $P(Y = 1) = 0.0064$ and a FAR value equal to

$$\{[0.0016 \cdot 2 + 0.0064 \cdot 1]/2 \cdot 8760\} \cdot 10^8 = 55,$$

assuming 8760 hours of exposure per year for two persons. Remember that the Fatal Accident Rate (FAR) value is defined as the expected number of fatalities per 100 million exposed hours.

6.7.1 Barrier block diagrams

There exist several alternative tools to event trees. Some of the examples are event sequence diagrams and barrier block diagrams. The former is much in use, for example, in the aviation and aerospace industries. We will not discuss it in any further detail in this book. Barrier diagrams are widely used, for example, in the Norwegian oil and gas industry. By this approach, initiating events, barrier functions and terminating events are shown along a horizontal line. The barrier systems are shown as boxes below this line; see the example in Figure 8.1. Barrier functions are functions to prevent the occurrence of an initiating event or to reduce the damage by interrupting an undesirable event sequence. Barrier systems are solutions that will ensure that the actual barrier function is carried out. One of the strengths of barrier block diagrams is that they clearly show the difference between barrier functions and barrier systems.

6.8   Bayesian networks

A Bayesian network consists of events (nodes) and arrows. The arrows indicate dependencies, that is, causal connections. Each node can be in various states; the

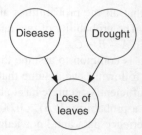

Figure 6.10   Example of a Bayesian network.

number of states is selected by the risk analyst. A Bayesian network is not limited to two states, as are event trees and fault trees. In a quantitative analysis, we must determine conditional probabilities for these states given the causal connections. This can be done by a direct argument or using some type of specified procedures. A simple Bayesian network is presented in Figure 6.10. This example will be used to explain what a Bayesian network is and how it is used. The example was obtained from the software supplier Hugin.

Example

John has an apple tree in the garden and one day he discovers that the tree is losing its leaves. He knows that apple trees can lose their leaves if they are not adequately watered. But it can also be an indication of a disease.

The network in Figure 6.10 models the causal links. The network consists of three nodes: disease, drought and loss of leaves. As a simplification, each node has two states only; the apple tree is either diseased or not, it is impacted by drought or not and it is either losing leaves or not. We see from the arrows in the Bayesian network that disease and drought are possible causes of the tree losing its leaves. It is common to use the designation 'parent' and 'child' for the two different levels of the nodes in the network. For the three nodes in the example, we will thus say that 'disease' and 'drought' are the parent nodes for 'loss of leaves'. A quantitative analysis requires that we specify the conditional probabilities. This is often done in tables called *CPT* or *Conditional Probability Tables*. The probabilities that the tree will lose leaves, given various combinations of disease and drought, are given in Table 6.6.

The probabilities could be based on available experience data or determined by expert judgements. All probabilities in Table 6.6 are conditioned on the state of the parent nodes. In addition, we need to specify the unconditional probabilities for disease and drought. Let us assume that John, after consulting a botanist, specifies a probability of 10% that the tree is diseased. He also assigns a probability of 10% that the tree is suffering from drought.

We have thus constructed a Bayesian network and established the probabilities for the various quantities (events) in the network. The task is now to calculate the

Table 6.6   Conditional probabilities.

	Drought = Yes		Drought = No	
	Disease = Yes %	Disease = No %	Disease = Yes %	Disease = No %
Loss of leaves = Yes	95	85	90	2
Loss of leaves = No	5	15	10	98

probability of the apple tree being diseased, given that we have observed that it is losing leaves, or in other words,

$$P(\text{diseased}|\text{loss of leaves}).$$

To find this probability, we make use of the so-called Bayes' formula. To simplify, we introduce events A, B and C, expressing disease (A), drought (B) and loss of leaves (C). The complementary events are denoted $\overline{A}$ and so on. The task is to compute $P(A|C)$.

Bayes' formula gives

$$P(A|C) = \frac{P(C|A)P(A)}{P(C)},$$

where $P(A)$ has been assigned the value 0.10. Hence, it remains to determine $P(C|A)$ and $P(C)$. Let us first look at $P(C|A)$.

The arrows in the Bayesian network show that in addition to being dependent on A, C is also dependent on B. Using the law of total probability, we can write

$$P(C|A) = P(C|A, B)P(B|A) + P(C|A, \overline{B})P(\overline{B}|A).$$

Assuming independence between A and B (in line with the network model shown in Figure 6.10), we obtain

$$P(C|A) = P(C|A, B)P(B) + P(C|A, \overline{B})P(\overline{B}) = 0.95 \cdot 0.1 + 0.9 \cdot 0.9$$

$$= 0.905.$$

Hence, according to Bayes' formula $P(A|C) \cdot P(C) = 0.905 \cdot 0.1$. Similarly, we obtain $P(\overline{A}|C) \cdot P(C) = 0.103 \cdot 0.9$, as

$$P(C|\overline{A}) = P(C|\overline{A}, B)P(B) + P(C|\overline{A}, \overline{B})P(\overline{B}) = 0.85 \cdot 0.1 + 0.02 \cdot 0.9$$

$$= 0.103.$$

By summing $P(A|C) \cdot P(C)$ and $P(\overline{A}|C) \cdot P(C)$, we obtain $P(C) = 0.905 \cdot 0.1 + 0.103 \cdot 0.9 = 0.1832$.

We can then compute the desired probability:

$$P(A|C) = \frac{P(C|A)P(A)}{P(C)} = \frac{0.905 \cdot 0.1}{0.183} = 0.494.$$

In other words, there is a 49% probability that the tree is diseased when we see that it is losing leaves.

Bayesian networks can be used for many types of applications, for example:

- *Shipping accidents*: Modelling of what causes the responsible officer on a ship to make an error leading to a collision. Factors such as the time of day, stress, experience, knowledge, shift arrangements and weather are factors that may be considered in the cause modelling.

- *Financial considerations*: Credit assessments of customers. Factors that are deemed to influence the capacity to pay, such as age and income, are modelled. In discussions with customers, individual nodes are locked, the model is updated and a probability of the customer not being able to pay within a given period is calculated.

- *Medicine*: Assistance in making diagnoses. A model for the relationship between various symptoms and analysis results is drawn up (once by experts within the profession). Subsequently, other physicians may submit analysis results and symptoms for individual patients into the model (lock some of the nodes) and calculate the probability of the patient having a disease or being healthy.

Bayesian networks have been regularly used in fields such as the aviation and aerospace industries, but have not been very common in, for example, the offshore industry. We see, however, that the method is becoming more and more commonly used in a number of different fields, such as offshore operations, health, transport, banking and financial areas.

Bayesian networks have been shown to be appropriate in connection with analyses of complex causal relationships. In risk analyses, however, there will always be a need for simple methods such as event and fault trees. Obviously, different situations call for different methods.

6.9   Monte Carlo simulation

Monte Carlo simulation represents an alternative to analytical calculation methods. The technique is to generate a computer model of the system to be investigated, for example, represented as a reliability block diagram, and then to simulate the operation of the system for a specific period of time. Using the computer, we generate realisations of the system performance. The sojourn times in the various states are determined by sampling from appropriate probability distributions. For example, for a two-state component, the operating times (uptimes) are sampled from a lifetime distribution and the downtimes are sampled from a repair time distribution. If T represents the lifetime of a component, the probability distribution $F(t)$ is given by $F(t) = P(T \leq t)$; see Appendix B. The system state is computed and logged as time elapses. For each realisation of the system performance, we can compute, for example, the uptime of the system. Simulating the system performance a number of times, say n times, we can estimate the probability distribution for the uptime and the probability p that the system is functioning at a particular point in time. For example, the probability p is estimated by the average value of the realisations where the system is functioning. By increasing n, the estimation error can be made negligible.

With a Monte Carlo simulation model, the time aspect is more easily handled than with an analytical method. A Monte Carlo simulation model may be a fairly good representation of the real world. This is one of the greatest attractions of Monte Carlo simulation over analytical methods.

Monte Carlo Simulation requires in general detailed input data. For example, the lifetime and repair time distributions must be specified. Mean values, as used in many analytical models, are not sufficient. On the other hand, the output from a Monte Carlo simulation model is very extensive and informative.

The main disadvantage of the Monte Carlo simulation technique compared with an analytical approach is the time and expense involved in the development and execution of the model. To obtain accurate results using simulation, a large number of trials is usually required, especially when the system is functioning most of the time. The time and expense aspect is very important if the model is to be used to study the effects of changes in system configurations, or if sensitivity analyses are to be performed.

With a complex Monte Carlo simulation model, it is difficult to check if the program has been written correctly and, therefore, if the result can be relied upon. For further details on Monte Carlo simulation, see Zio (2013).

7

Safety measures for a road tunnel

Let us look back at the problem introduced in Section 1.3.1. A risk analysis is to be carried out to predict the effect of various alternative safety measures for a road tunnel. The analysis, together with other relevant information, will be used as the basis for the decision-making concerning what measure(s) to implement.

7.1 Planning

7.1.1 Problem definition

What are the consequences of a ventilation system not being able to handle a 100-MW fire? The aim of the fire ventilation system is to ensure that the smoke gases are forced away from the fire site and directed further inwards into the tunnel section, in the direction of traffic flow. For a dual carriageway tunnel, this is advantageous as the drivers situated downstream of (past) the fire site will exit the tunnel without even being aware of the existence of the fire. The cars that are located upstream of (before) the fire site will have to stop when they encounter the fire or smoke, thus forming a queue. In such a situation, it is important to force the smoke gases further inwards into the tunnel and thus avoid the situation whereby the drivers stationary in the queue upstream of the fire are exposed to smoke gases before they can evacuate on foot out of the tunnel or through the cross galleries (emergency exits).

The case is based on a tunnel that is almost horizontal. There is a slight rise in one carriageway and a slight fall in the other carriageway. Because warm air is lighter than cold air, the hot fire gases will create updraft forces, which will cause the smoke

---

Risk Analysis, Second Edition. Terje Aven.
© 2015 John Wiley & Sons, Ltd. Published 2015 by John Wiley & Sons, Ltd.

to rise. In the upward-sloping tunnel carriageway, this does not represent a problem as the updraft forces will draw the smoke in the desirable direction. However, in the downward-sloping tunnel carriageway, the smoke will tend to move in the wrong direction. In such cases, it is the job of the fire ventilation system to 'force' the smoke gases downwards in the carriageway and away from the fire site, in the direction of traffic flow. The actual ventilation system in the tunnel example is designed to blow the smoke gases in the right direction in the event of a 20-MW fire, but not in the case of a 100-MW fire.

The objective of the risk analysis is to address the following questions:

- What will be the safety-related effect of an upgrade of the fire ventilation system to be able to handle a 100-MW fire?

- What will be the safety-related effect of other compensating measures?

The speed at which the smoke will spread in the wrong direction and the consequences this will have for drivers will be studied in the risk analysis (see Section 7.2.3).

The risk description covers (A, C, P, K) using the notation from Chapter 2. In this case, the focus will be placed on vulnerability, that is, the possible consequences, along with the associated uncertainty, if a fire or some other hazardous situation occurs in the tunnel.

7.1.2   Selection of analysis method

A coarse risk analysis method, based on expert meetings, was first applied. In this method, possible safety measures were identified and the effects of these were qualitatively described. In the meetings, the risk analysts were joined by experts in the fields of road tunnels, ventilation and fires. The problem required considerable technical competence in these fields. On the basis of the qualitative analysis, the risk analysts carried out a quantitative risk analysis, expressing the effect of suggested safety measures on risk. The results are presented along with the assumptions and suppositions made. The risk analysis method can be regarded as a simple form of model-based risk analysis, adapted to the problem being considered.

The analysis is relatively simple and basic. A more sophisticated method, for example, based on Bayesian networks could have also been used. In that case, we could have described, in a more nuanced manner, the relationship between the various variables (traffic volume, smoke, fire, fatalities, etc.). However, carrying out this type of analysis would have been more resource demanding. The method selected is deemed to be sufficient for the objectives defined. The main point is to identify and describe the main features of the risks and vulnerabilities.

7.2 Risk assessment

7.2.1 Identification of initiating events

The aim of the hazard identification is to determine which undesirable events are influenced by the fact that the fire ventilation system is dimensioned for a 20-MW fire, and not for a 100-MW one, as is required by the present regulations.

The analysis begins with a listing of the common undesirable events related to road tunnels as shown in Table 7.1 (based on Norwegian Public Roads Administration, 2007).

The analysis group also considers other possible undesirable events. The group concluded that

> The design of the fire ventilation system has importance only for the undesirable event – fire.

The fire event can, however, lead to a large spectrum of different scenarios. A fire near a tunnel opening will be completely different from a fire midway in the tunnel.

Table 7.1   List of typical undesirable events at different specification levels.

Traffic accidents		Light vehicles
	Head-on collisions	Light vs. heavy vehicles
		Heavy vehicles
	Rear-end crash	Light vehicles
		Light vehicle struck by heavy vehicle
	Crashes involving non-motorists	Following vehicle breakdown, for example
	Driving off the road	Wall, verge, ramps, etc.
	Lane-changing accidents	
Fire	Small fire (5 MW)	Fire in light vehicles
	Large fire (>20 MW)	Fire in heavy vehicles
Leakage of hazardous goods	Petrol	
	Toxic substances	
Vehicle stoppage	Light vehicles	
	Heavy vehicles	
Overturn	Buses	Especially tall buses, house
	Other heavy vehicles	trailers and tractor trailers with a high centre of gravity

Likewise, the consequences of a fire in the downward-sloping tunnel carriageway will, as mentioned earlier, be more serious than a similar fire in the upward-sloping carriageway. In order to reflect this spectrum, the analysis group chooses to differentiate between the following scenarios:

- Scenario 1: Fire approximately midway in the tunnel, carriageway with uphill slope.

- Scenario 2: Fire approximately midway in the tunnel, carriageway with downhill slope.

- Scenario 3: Fire approximately midway in carriageway with downhill slope; queue present in the entire carriageway. before fire breaks out

- Scenario 4: Fire 200 m into the tunnel, carriageway with uphill slope.

- Scenario 5: Fire 200 m before the end of the tunnel, carriageway with downhill slope.

Scenario 3 reflects the fact that sometimes there may be a queue present when the fire breaks out. In such situations, there will be queues in the tunnel both upstream and downstream of the fire. This means that the ventilation system will blow smoke against those who are waiting in the queue just past the fire site.

During the expert meetings, the effect of the various alternative safety measures was assessed qualitatively. The following measures were assessed:

- Upgrading of the ventilation system in accordance with the regulatory requirements.

- Installation of a fire detection cable in the ceiling of the tunnel. This is a system that sends a message to the road traffic central notifying them of a fire in the tunnel when the ceiling temperature reaches 67 °C. The central could then take measures to close off the tunnel with a barrier across the entrance, start up the fire ventilation system and alert the local fire department that there is a fire in the tunnel.

- Installation of event detection equipment inside the tunnel. This may be a video camera–based system that automatically senses changes in the traffic situation and sounds an alarm at the road traffic central and automatically 'freezes' the video picture. In this way, the operator can clearly see what is happening in the tunnel and can initiate measures such as closing down the tunnel, closing off a lane, reducing the speed limit and sending out a call for intervention personnel. Examples of events that are automatically detected are fire, vehicle breakdown (stationary vehicle), objects on the roadway, animals or pedestrians in the tunnel and traffic accidents.

7.2.2   Cause analysis

The risk analysis focuses on risk-reducing measures, assuming a fire of 100 MW. Fire is defined as the undesirable event. Hence, the analysis focuses attention on the vulnerabilities related to such an event, that is, the consequence side of Figure 1.1. There is no need for a cause analysis to provide decision-making support for this decision problem. This does not mean that the cause side is not important when it comes to risk reduction. One would, of course, take every precaution so that fires and other undesirable events do not occur in the tunnel. However, for the present decision-making problem, this is not the main issue. The requirement for the new regulations assumes the occurrence of a fire of 100 MW.

7.2.3   Consequence analysis

The consequence analysis is the most important part of the risk analysis process. What will happen if a 100-MW fire breaks out at a given site in the tunnel? In order to answer this question, detailed consequence simulations are carried out, using a computer software tool based on CFD modelling. The simulations show how a fire in the tunnel evolves into a 100-MW fire (assuming a realistic sequence of events).

Next, we need to take into account the number of people in the tunnel, where they are situated, evacuation time and so on. A large number of scenarios are possible. There is normally less traffic at night than during the day, and it is conceivable that the fire occurs when a bus full of wheel-chair users just happen to be on the scene. In practice, however, we cannot take all such situations into account. Simplifications must be made. The analysis must select dimensioning events and scenarios, and it will be based on a variety of conditions and assumptions. Five main scenarios are considered as mentioned in Section 7.2.1.

The people in the tunnel are categorised as shown in Figure 7.1. In the case of a fire in the tunnel, the people in the cars situated downstream of the fire (Group 1 in the figure) will normally drive out of the tunnel without being aware of what has happened. This assumes that there is no queue in the tunnel when the fire breaks out. If there is a queue in the tunnel when the fire breaks out, it is possible that Group 1 will have to leave their cars and evacuate by means of the cross gallery between the two carriageways. In order to differentiate between these situations, it may be appropriate to subdivide Group 1 into subgroups: G1W (walking) and G1D (driving). Since the tunnel cannot be closed before the road traffic central is aware that there is a fire, there will normally be many cars entering the tunnel upstream of the fire. These cars will form a queue upstream of the fire site. Those near the fire site (Group 2) will see the fire and will therefore evacuate on their own accord, except for those who are stuck within the vehicles. Those who are farther away from the fire site (Group 3) will normally not evacuate before they are requested to do so or before they see the smoke coming towards them, as they are not aware that the queue is being caused by a fire. As far as the ventilation is concerned, the groups have different requirements:

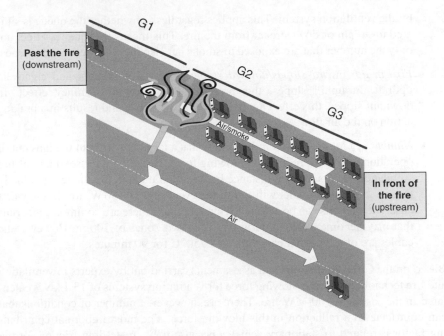

Figure 7.1   Categorisation of people in the tunnel.

- Group 1: For this group, it is desirable, in principle, to have as little ventilation as possible. This is particularly the case if there is a queue present in the tunnel when the event occurs because the groups must then evacuate on foot.

- Group 2: For this group, it is desirable to have enough ventilation to provide good visibility for the evacuation. Maximum distance to the first cross gallery is 250 m. It normally takes 4 minutes to cover this distance and the time taken to make the decision to evacuate.

- Group 3: This group is not really affected by the event (but the ventilation affects the size of Group 2 compared to Group 3). If they do not evacuate, they can also be exposed to smoke after a while.

What influences the spread of smoke?

The following conditions affect the blowing force of the ventilation system:

- *Headwind*: This means that the wind is blowing in the direction opposite to the traffic flow and, because of this, has a braking effect on the air flow in the tunnel.

- *Queue*: Stationary cars. A queue affects the ventilation rate in that stationary traffic creates a certain amount of drag on the air flow created through the tunnel by the ventilation system. This applies regardless of whether the queue is situated upstream or downstream from the fire. This means that queues affect not only the number that are exposed to smoke but also the way the smoke spreads.

- *Fire in downward slopes/upward slopes*: Fire gases are hot and create an updraft. In uphill slopes, this produces the so-called chimney effect. In downhill slopes, this effect applies in a negative sense and results in a braking action on the air flow.

- *Number of fans in operation*: It is likely that a large fire will put the fans out of operation. This will reduce the blowing force. Based on an assessment of fire simulation results and the distance between fan units in the tunnel, it is likely that up to three fan units will fail in the event of a 100-MW fire. In the worst case, six fan units can be affected. This is because there are common cable runs that may become exposed during a fire in two zones of 300 m. However, the cables are of a type that can withstand 750 °C for 90 minutes.

Based on the CFD simulations and assessments carried out by experts in ventilation and fire technology, a gross blowing force for ventilation systems of 13.1 kN is calculated in the case of a 100-MW fire. There are, however, a number of conditions that can contribute to a reduction in this blowing force. The most important contributing factor is related to stationary vehicles because they create drag friction for the air-flow stream. The next most important contributor is the fire itself if it occurs in the carriageway having a slight downhill slope. In a 100-MW fire, the effect of the fire on the ventilation is equal to that of a 50% queue. If there is a 100% queue, this would affect the blowing force twice as much as the fire itself. The fire also affects the number of fans in operation (in that they can be put out of operation), and this contributes in a negative way to the blowing force.

To summarise, a queue in the tunnel has a greater effect on the blowing force of the ventilation system than the fire itself, assuming a fire of 100 MW. This is an important observation – it means that measures that lead to rapid closing of the tunnel can be more effective, insofar as the blowing force is concerned, than upgrading of the ventilation system. A rapid closure results in a smaller queue. Fires introduce vulnerability, in that it is likely that two to three fans will fail. However, this applies regardless of whether the fans are upgraded or not.

The above consequence analysis addresses the physical conditions in the tunnel in the event of a fire. What are the consequences then in terms of fatalities and severely injured?

Based on the expert meetings and the knowledge obtained from the above studies, the risk analysts assess each scenario for all the alternative safety measures. Using event detection equipment, it will be possible to close the tunnel quickly since the event is being monitored from the road traffic central. Quick closure would lead to fewer vehicles entering the tunnel, which would in turn reduce the queue upstream of the fire. This would also affect the ventilation rate and thus the development of the smoke dispersion. The result is likely to be a reduced number of fatalities and severely injured, in comparison to the status quo. The risk analysts conclude that event detection equipment will be more effective than fire detection cables, since the operator monitoring the event detection equipment in the road traffic central will receive an immediate, automatic alarm and would be able to look at once at the video screens that show what is happening. Thus, he/she would be able to make a decision immediately to initiate the closure. In the case of fire detection cables, the message to the operator is more ambiguous, which can lead to more time being taken to clarify the situation and thus a longer time before closure. This leads to more vehicles in the queue upstream of the fire and thus reduced blowing force, compared with using event detection equipment.

Table 7.2 shows an example of the result of these assessments for the scenario in which no additional safety measures are implemented. Note that retaining the tunnel as it was originally planned is not acceptable with regard to the regulatory requirements, but we still analyse the 'status quo' in the risk analysis to be able to compare the effect of the various safety measures.

The analysis in this case is relatively crude. Average figures are used for a number of quantities included in the analysis, for example, traffic volume. Furthermore, conditions that can cause large deviations between the expected values and the actual number of fatalities and injured are discussed. Let us look at examples related to Scenario 3: fire approximately midway in tunnel, queue in entire tunnel (before fire breaks out).

In this case, the expected number of fatalities and severely injured is 100, assuming the ventilation system is upgraded. The actual number in such a scenario can, however, be both much higher and much lower. If the fire knocks out a number of fans, and there is, in addition, a large number of people in the tunnel, for example, as a result of a number of buses with tourists being in the tunnel, the number of persons impacted can be much greater than 100. The uncertainties in the number of fatalities are significant.

7.2.4   Risk picture

Table 7.3 shows the main results obtained for the various scenarios expressed as the expected number of fatalities and severely injured in the event of a large fire.

The results also highlight the factors contributing to the risk and key assumptions made in the analysis. In addition, factors that can cause large deviations compared to the expected values are discussed. This relates, for example, to the number of fatalities. What type of scenarios could lead to high number of fatalities, and how likely is it that these scenarios would occur? Furthermore, sensitivities are presented showing the effect of changes in the assumptions. Strength of knowledge assessment could have been conducted in line with the ideas presented in Section 2.4.

Table 7.2   Examples of assumptions made in the risk analysis.

Expected number of fatalities or severely injured – no additional risk-reducing measures	G1W	G1D	G3	G2	Comments
Scenario 2: fire approximately midway in carriageway with downhill slope, no queue present when fire breaks out.	0	0	1	10	G1: no fatalities or severe injuries as it is assumed that all cars could drive out. G2: 10 fatalities or severely injured. People stuck in vehicles taken into account. Also taken into account the fact that some people did not understand the seriousness of the situation before it was too late. G3: smoke will travel at a quick walking pace. One person in this zone is assumed to be killed or severely injured.

Table 7.3   Results from the risk analysis.

Expected number of fatalities or severely injured in a 100-MW fire	Without any measures taken	Upgrading of fire ventilation system	Event detection system	Fire detection cable
Scenario 1: midway in tunnel, carriageway with uphill slope	3.0	3.0	2.5	3.0
Scenario 2: midway in tunnel, carriageway with downhill slope	11	3.0	3.5	10
Scenario 3: midway in tunnel, queue in entire tunnel (before fire breaks out)	91	100	77	85
Scenario 4: close to the entrance (200 m inside)	2.5	2.5	2.3	2.5
Scenario 5: close to the exit (200 m before exit)	11	3.0	6.5	10

7.3   Risk treatment

7.3.1   Comparison of alternatives

Based on the overall risk picture obtained, it is concluded that event detection would be the best measure and that this measure is much better than upgrading of the fire ventilation system (which is now required by regulations). The event detection will facilitate quick closing of the tunnel, thus ensuring that few vehicles could then enter. In this way, the queue upstream of the fire is reduced, which is favourable from a ventilation point of view. In general, this measure results in the lowest expected number of fatalities and severely injured. In addition, the uncertainty factors are in favour of such a measure. Furthermore, the measure will reduce the probability of traffic accidents as the tunnel or the driving lane can be closed and the speed limit lowered in the case of breakdowns, objects on the roadway and so on.

7.3.2   Management review and decision

Based on the results from the risk analysis and a more comprehensive assessment of the costs and the consequences the various measures have with respect to temporary closure of the tunnel, the tunnel owner chooses to install event detection equipment in the tunnel as an alternative to upgrading the ventilation system. The analysis is used as formal documentation to demonstrate that this measure will provide considerably greater risk reduction than the regulation-imposed measure. The authorities pose a number of critical questions regarding the risk assessment and its basis (assumptions and suppositions). The process ends with the authorities concluding the judgement of the risk analysis being reasonable and accepting the deviation from the regulations.

The example shows that risk analysis is used in supporting the decision-making. Event detection was deemed to be the best measure overall, when the advantages and disadvantages of the alternative measures were assessed. Following this, a decision was made to choose this measure, despite the fact that the regulation requirement was that another measure should be implemented.

8

Risk analysis process for an offshore installation

A risk analysis is to be carried out for an offshore installation. The installation is part of a so-called production complex, that is, bridge-linked installations. The installation in question is a production platform. The scope of the case is a significant modification of the installation, implying adding new production equipment, which will have an impact on the risk level. New equipment units will imply additional potential leak sources, with respect to gas and/or oil leaks, which may cause fire and/or explosion, if ignited. The decision to be made is whether or not to install additional fire protection for the personnel in order to reduce the consequences in the event of fires on the installation.

The installation has been designed with rather limited protection of personnel during the use of escape ways against fire and explosion effects. The installation has an important function at the field as the only installation to process oil and gas from the field. The operation is expected to continue for the next 20 years. The example is based on Aven (2008).

8.1 Planning

8.1.1 Problem definition

Following a review of the problem, it was quickly evident that one was faced with three alternatives:

1. Minor improvement in order to compensate for increased risk due to new equipment, but no further risk reduction.

---

2. Installation of protective shielding on existing escape ways together with overpressure protection in order to avoid smoke ingress into the enclosed escape ways.

3. Do nothing, accept situation as is.

The objective of the risk analysis is to provide a basis for selecting an alternative. This basis consists of a risk description and associated evaluation. The description covers (A, C, P, K), using the notation from Chapter 2. The analysis group will identify hazards A, express uncertainty using probabilities P and describe the (strength) of the background knowledge K.

The work is carried out by a group of risk analysts. The group has in-depth competence within the fields of fire and explosion.

8.1.2   Selection of analysis method

A model-based analysis is used in this case. The problem to be addressed is considered important by both the management and employees, and in order to provide a good basis for the decision to be made, a thorough and detailed analysis providing an informative risk picture is necessary.

The analysis places emphasis on both qualitative and quantitative aspects and will form part of an As Low As Reasonably Practicable (ALARP) process.

8.2   Risk analysis

8.2.1   Hazard identification

The analysis focuses on hydrocarbon leakages.

8.2.2   Cause analysis

What does it take for a leakage to occur? An extensive body of statistics is available on leakages on offshore installations, and this also gives a picture of the most important causes of leakage. A significant proportion of the leakages are linked to manual operations. An example of a cause analysis for such an operation is shown in Figure 8.1. The initiating event is 'a valve in the wrong position after maintenance'. To analyse the actual barriers, a fault tree is constructed as illustrated in Figure 8.2.

The probabilities for the events in these diagrams are affected by a set of risk-influencing factors and influence diagrams (Bayesian networks) can be used to show these effects. An example for the basic event 'operator does not detect the valve to be in a wrong position during self-control/use of checklist' is shown in Figure 8.3.

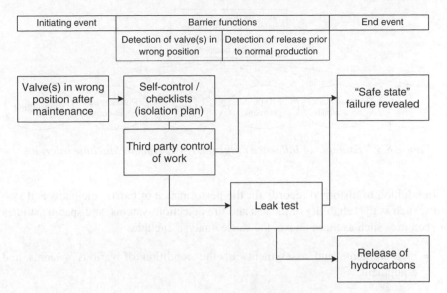

Initiating event	Barrier functions		End event
	Detection of valve(s) in wrong position	Detection of release prior to normal production	

Figure 8.1   Barrier block diagram.

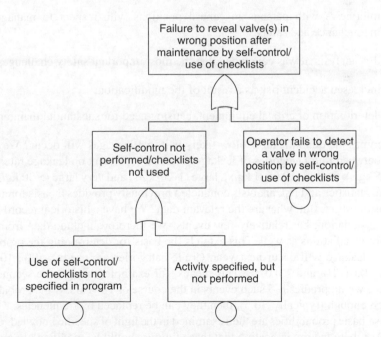

Figure 8.2   Fault tree for failure of a barrier.

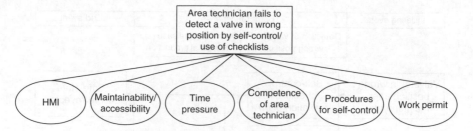

Figure 8.3   Example of influence diagram. HMI: Human Machine Interface.

In addition to historical records for the performance of barrier elements and systems, such as the reliability of the gas and fire detection systems, and specific studies of scenarios such as those above, the cause analysis includes

- measurements and assessments of the condition of various systems and equipment;

- results from accident investigations and reports;

- assessment of the performance of important barriers; and

- interviews with persons in central positions with respect to management, maintenance and safety.

From this analysis, it was concluded that the most important safety challenges were

- increased accident risk as a result of the modification;

- deterioration of critical equipment, causing need for substantial maintenance.

Next comes the quantification. How likely is it that leakages will occur? We distinguish between four categories of leakages that are dependent on leakage rate: minor (<0.05 kg/s), medium (0.05–1 kg/s), large (1–30 kg/s) and very large (>30 kg/s). The leakage statistics and risk analysis conducted previously provides a basis for answering this question. But, what are the relevant data? We have a historical record for the actual installation, but relatively few events. We therefore include data from other offshore installations as well. This extends the basis for determining the probability p that a leakage will occur next year. Crude categories are used: >50%, 10–50%, 1–10%, 0.01–1% and <0.01%. This means, for example, that for the second category, we would predict 1–5 such events in the course of 10 years. If the probabilities are high enough (typically >0.5), then they can be replaced by frequencies.

These basic probabilities are then examined in the light of specific knowledge available. Are there factors indicating that these figures should be modified? In our case, equipment deterioration was identified as a problem, but the probabilities were not adjusted. Instead, an assumption was made that a comprehensive maintenance programme will be carried out.

The effect of the modification was assessed and the relevant probabilities adjusted. An example of a probability that was quantified is: increased probability of 5% for leakage in category medium.

8.2.3 Consequence analysis

If a leakage should occur, various consequences could result. The event development is analysed with the aid of an event tree. An example is shown in Figure 8.4.

The analysis addresses the main barrier functions:

- Prevent ignition

- Reduce cloud/emissions

- Prevent escalation

- Prevent fatalities.

Specific studies are carried out for these barrier functions analogous, in principle, to the barrier function 'prevent loss of containment (leakage)'. We write 'analogous, in principle' because, in practice, there are differences in the methodology. The database is, naturally, significantly smaller for barriers after leakage has occurred, so there is a greater need for modelling and analysis of these barriers.

A set of scenarios are defined, and for these consequences, calculations are carried out providing insights about, for example, initial release rates and development

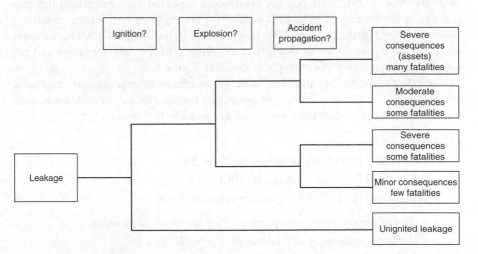

Figure 8.4   Accident development modelled using an event tree.

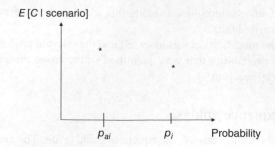

Figure 8.5   Risk description showing the probability of occurrence of two scenarios and the associated expected number of fatalities.

of the discharge concentration (when and where we could get a combustible mixture). From these studies and the analysis group's general risk analysis experience, the uncertainties related to releases and consequences are assessed. The assessments are based on all relevant information, including the identified poor performance of some of the safety barriers and the equipment deterioration problem. The consecutive assigned probabilities and expected values represent the analyst group's best judgements, based on the available information and knowledge (K).

In addition to the probability of leakage, we are especially interested in the probability that an ignited leakage, that is, a fire or an explosion, will occur. Next, focus will be placed on the probability of accident spreading and potential injuries and fatalities.

Let C represent the number of fatalities. In the analysis, the probability of a fatal accident, that is, $P(C > 0)$, and the conditional expected number of fatalities in a leakage or fire scenario, that is, $E[C|$ scenario $i]$, are expressed. Risk is quantitatively described based on the pair: ($p_i, E[C|$ leak scenario $i]$) and ($p_{ai}, E[C|$ fire scenario $i]$). Here, p_i and p_{ai} equal the probability of occurrence of the leak scenario i and fire scenario i, respectively. An example is shown in Figure 8.5.

The effect of the modification was analysed, and the relevant probabilities updated. Also, the effect of implementing fire protection for the evacuation routes was analysed. Examples of probabilities quantified are given as follows:

- Modification
  - Increased probability of ignited leakage: 5%
  - Increased Potential Loss of Life (PLL): 5%
  - Increased IR: 10% for a specific personnel group.

- Effect of implementing fire protection for the evacuation routes
  - Reduced probability of fatalities $P(C > 0)$: 30%
  - Reduced PLL: 30%
  - Reduced IR: 50% for specific personnel groups.

Uncertainty (knowledge) assessments

- *Equipment deterioration and maintenance*: The deterioration of critical equipment is assumed not to cause safety problems by implementing a special maintenance programme. However, experience gained on offshore installations indicates that unexpected problems do occur. Production of oil over time leads to changes in operating conditions, such as increased production of water, H_2S and CO_2 content, scaling, bacterial growth and emulsions; problems that, to a large extent, need to be solved by the addition of chemicals. These are all factors causing increased probability of corrosion, material brittleness and other conditions that may cause leakages. The quantitative analysis has not taken into account that surprises might occur. The analysis group is concerned about this uncertainty factor, and it is reported along with the quantitative analysis.

- *Barrier performance*: The historical records show poor performance of a set of critical safety barrier elements, in particular, for some types of safety valves. The assignments of the expected number of fatalities given a leakage or a fire scenario were based on average conditions for the safety barriers and adjustments were made to reflect the historical records. However, the changes made were small. The poor performance of the barrier elements would not necessarily result in significant reduced probabilities of barrier system failures, as most of the barrier elements are not safety critical elements. The barrier systems are designed with a lot of redundancies. Nonetheless, this problem causes concern, as the poor performance may indicate that there is an underlying problem of operational and maintenance character, which results in reduced availability of the safety barriers in a hazardous situation. There are a number of dependencies among elements in these systems, and the risk analysis methods for studying these are simplified with strong limitations. Hence, there is also an uncertainty aspect related to the barrier performance.

Based on these and some other judgements, the strength of knowledge supporting the quantitative analysis is given a medium score.

8.3   Risk picture and comparison of alternatives

The results from the analysis are summarised in Tables 8.1 and 8.2. The investment cost for the fire protection is €5 million. Can this extra cost be justified?

To determine the appropriate category in Table 8.2, the two-stage procedure outlined in Chapter 2 was used. To obtain a high score (significant or serious), the factor must be judged as important for the risk indices considered and the factor must be subject to large uncertainties.

The expected reduced number of fatalities is rather small, and hence, the expected cost per expected number of saved lives (the implied value of a statistical life) would give a rather high number, and a traditional cost–benefit (cost-effectiveness) criterion would not justify the measure. Say that the assigned expected reduced

Table 8.1   Result summary for the risk analysis. Overall assessments of modification and measures.

Modification	The resultant fire risk is not deemed to present any great problem, the risk increases by 5%
Fire protection implemented	Relative large improvements in risks (30%) Reduced IR by 50% for specific personnel group

Table 8.2   Result summary for the risk analysis. Uncertainty factors.

Uncertainty factors	Minor problem	Significant problem	Serious problem
Deterioration of equipment		x	
Barrier performance	x		

number of fatalities is 0.1. Then, we obtain an implied value of a statistical life equal to $5/0.1 = €50$ million. If this number is considered in isolation, in a quantitative context, it would normally be considered too high to justify the implementation of the measure.

But, the risk management perspective here is broader. The objective of investing in the measure is to reduce risk and uncertainty, and the traditional cost–benefit analysis (cost-effectiveness analysis) does not reflect these concerns in a satisfactory way. The sensitivity analysis shows that changes in the key assumptions and numerical values can result in a much lower figure for an implied statistical life. However, the argumentation should not be based only on this type of analysis. The important question is how we weigh the uncertainties. Uncertainty in phenomena and processes justifies investments in safety measures.

8.4   Management review and judgement

So, what will be the conclusion? Should fire protection be installed? This depends on the attitude of management towards risk and uncertainties. The analysis does not provide a clear answer. If management places emphasis on the cautionary principle, then the investment in fire protection can be justified, despite the fact that a traditional cost–benefit consideration indicates that the measure cannot be justified.

Reflection

How does this example show that it is necessary to look beyond the calculated probabilities?

The probabilities are conditioned on certain factors, and thus, considerable uncertainty can be hidden. It is assumed, for example, that the maintenance effort will be so effective that the equipment deterioration will not present any significant problem.

9

Production assurance

A production system in a processing plant is to be designed. Two alternative systems are being considered: S_I and S_{II}. Alternative S_I consists of one production line, while alternative S_{II} has two lines a and b. To provide a basis for choosing an alternative, an analysis is carried out, calculating the expected production and risk.

9.1 Planning

The analysis should provide a nuanced description of risk, that is, a description that covers (A, C, P, K), with reference to the terminology introduced in Chapter 2. The analysis may be alternatively referred to as a *production assurance analysis*, or a *production availability analysis* (ISO 2008, Hjorteland et al. 2007, Aven and Pedersen 2014).

A model-based analysis is used in this case. The investment in the two production lines is significant, and management requires a solid decision-making basis. In this case, the example has been much simplified, to allow for simple hand calculations. For more comprehensive cases, Monte Carlo simulations (see Section 6.9) could be used.

9.2 Risk analysis

9.2.1 Identification of failures

An FMEA is carried out to obtain an overview of what types of failures can arise in the system and what the consequences of these could be. Examples of failure events are technical failure of various types of equipment, failure in the ancillary systems such as the power supply and accident events.

Risk Analysis, Second Edition. Terje Aven.
© 2015 John Wiley & Sons, Ltd. Published 2015 by John Wiley & Sons, Ltd.

9.2.2   Cause analysis

The causes of the failures are not studied in the analysis. The challenge is to model the system quite accurately to reflect, in a satisfactory way, the differences in the production between the two alternatives.

9.2.3   Consequence analysis

If a failure occurs, what will be the consequences for production? Two models are introduced to describe the consequences of failures for the two alternatives (see Figure 9.1). For alternative S_I, the model states that the production, Y_I, is given as follows:

$$Y_I = \min\{X_1, X_2, X_3\},$$

where X_i is the state (capacity) of equipment unit i, that is, Y_I is the state of the unit having the lowest capacity. The capacities of the three units are shown in Table 9.1.

All the units have two levels. If unit 1 or 3 fails, the capacity becomes 0. If unit 2 fails, the capacity is 40. If all the units function as intended, the capacity will be 100 for all units and for the system.

For alternative S_{II}, the following model is established:

$$Y_{II} = \min\{X_1, X_2, X_{3a} + X_{3b}\},$$

where the capacities are as shown in Table 9.2. See also Figure 9.1.

If both units 3a and 3b are functioning, the capacity will be 100, but if one of these two units fails, the capacity would be reduced to 80. The models are referred to as *flow networks*.

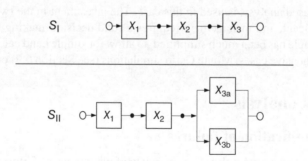

Figure 9.1   Flow network models for alternatives S_I and S_{II}.

Table 9.1   Capacity of the equipment units, alternative S_I.

Equipment unit	1	2	3
Capacity	0, 100	40, 100	0, 100

Table 9.2   Capacity of the equipment units, alternative S_{II}.

Equipment unit	1	2	3a	3b
Capacity	0, 100	40, 100	0, 80	0, 80

Table 9.3   Unavailabilities for the equipment.

Equipment unit	1	2	3	3a	3b
Unavailability (%)	5	5	10	10	10

Table 9.4   Expected production for alternatives S_I and S_{II}.

	Expected production
Alternative S_I	82
Alternative S_{II}	88

Next, we would like to assess the differences in the expected production for the two alternatives. If unit 3 fails, the production will come to a complete stop, but a failure in unit 3a or 3b will only give a 20% loss. The availability figures in Table 9.3 indicate how much of the time the units are assessed not to function over a long time horizon.

What will then be the availabilities for the two system alternatives S_I and S_{II}?

For S_I, it will be close to 80%, that is, 80% of the time production would be 100, 5% of the time it would be 40 and 15% it would be 0. This follows intuitively and can also be established using probability calculus: For the system to be in state 100, all the units must be functioning. The probabilities for this are 0.95, 0.95 and 0.90. If we multiply these figures, we find an availability of 0.81, which is approximately equal to 80%. The units are assumed to operate independently of each other.

For S_{II}, we arrive at the following figures: The system is in state 100 about 70% of the time, in state 80 about 20% of the time and in state 40 and 0, about 5% of the time for each. We illustrate the calculations by considering the case with 20%. Noting that the capacity 80 can result either when process line a or b fails, and each of these has a failure probability of 10%, we obtain a combined probability of 20%. This is only an approximation because we are ignoring the possibility of both lines being down at the same time.

We then calculate the expected production for both alternatives to obtain the results shown in Table 9.4.

Operating costs are calculated to be slightly larger for alternative S_{II} than for S_I. Alternative S_{II} has more equipment and the total failure frequency is slightly larger. The difference in expected discounted operational costs for the two alternatives is relatively small in relation to the expected production value. Operating costs are thus assumed not to be decisive when it comes to the selection of the best alternative. More important, however, is that alternative S_{II} has a higher safety risk. More failure and production stoppages increase the probability that fatal accidents or injuries will occur. It is difficult, however, to express this difference, but a rough analysis gives the following conclusions.

The leakage frequency per year is a factor of two larger for alternative S_{II} than for alternative S_{I}. This increases the probability for a fatal accident from 0.2% to about 0.4%.

Uncertainty assessments

There are a number of conditions that can cause a production that deviates considerably from the expected values:

- The equipment fails less frequently (more often) than expected.

- The preventive maintenance is more (less) effective than expected.

- A serious accident occurs.

- The analysis method has neglected important aspects.

An expected production difference of 6 is computed. This difference may be reduced if the equipment fails less often than expected and the preventive maintenance is more effective than expected. Efforts in these areas will thus give a smaller difference. On the other hand, more failures and less effective maintenance will give larger differences.

An example of a method-related aspect is the handling of independence and so-called common-mode failures (a failure that causes both lines not to function). In the analysis, such common-cause failures were not taken into account, as they were assumed not to have any great impact on the results. This assumption represents, however, an uncertainty factor. If we take into account the contribution of a common failure mode, the result will be a lower-than-expected production for alternative S_{II}.

9.3   Risk picture and comparison of alternatives

The results of the analysis are presented in Section 9.2. The difference in investment costs for the two alternatives is €30 million, as alternative S_{II} with its two production lines has a higher cost than S_{I}. A cost–benefit analysis with a basis of 10 years of production and a discount rate of 10% is carried out for the two alternatives, and it gives a difference in the expected present value of €7 million, in favour of alternative S_{II}. The earnings from the increased production are larger than the increased investment.

If we had extended the time horizon, the difference in favour of alternative S_{II} would have increased even further. This analysis has not take into consideration the difference in safety and the uncertainty factors discussed in the previous section. If we set the value of a statistical life at €10 million and we assume that the difference in PLL for the two alternatives is 0.05, then the expected discounted costs will be reduced by €0.5 million per year. Over a 10-year period, this will add up to €5 million. We see that the difference between the alternatives becomes reduced, and taking into account the precision level of the analysis and the quantification, we conclude that the two alternatives are approximately just as good. Here also, we have reflected the fact that uncertainty and risk are not given adequate weight in the cost–benefit analysis.

An aspect that has not been previously discussed is the possibility of increasing production. This possibility is regarded as being more realistic in the case of the two production lines than the one with one production line. If emphasis is placed on this aspect, the choice falls on alternative S_{II}. If weight is given to the cautionary principle with respect to safety, then alternative S_I will be selected.

9.4   Management review and judgement. Decision

What the conclusion will be depends on how the various aspects are weighted, as underlined above and in the previous example.

Reflection

Even if one does not place emphasis on all the figures in the analysis above, the calculations still contribute to a better insight into the problem. Do you have any comments regarding this statement? Do you agree?

We agree. Equally important to the number-crunching exercise is the structure that is created in terms of clarification of the problem and in elucidating the important factors.

10

Risk analysis process for a cash depot

We return to the problem described in Section 1.3.3. A risk analysis is to be conducted for the NOKAS facility. How should this be done? How should the analysis be planned, executed and used?

Our starting point is the description of the analysis (the analysis process) as carried out in 2005 (Vatn 2007). We have, however, made some adjustments, to be in line with the principles adopted in this book. The presentation shows only excerpts from the analysis; it is simplified, and all the figures have been changed. We refer the reader to the discussion at the end of the chapter for some comments regarding the differences between our presentation and the original analysis.

10.1 Planning

10.1.1 Problem definition

NOKAS, owned by Norges Bank (the Central Bank of Norway), DnB (the Norwegian Bank) and others, moved in May 2005 into new facilities located at Gausel, close to Stavanger. The area where the building is located is called *Frøystad*. The area is zoned for industry, but NOKAS has as its closest neighbour a cooperative kindergarten – and is also located close to a residential area. Prior to the move by NOKAS, the local municipality imposed an order on the enterprise to draw up a community safety plan for third parties (third persons) in the area, including report on perceived risks. Several analyses and reviews of the risks were then carried out. We will not look closer into these analyses here; our focus is the way we should plan, execute and use the risk

---

analysis according to the perspective introduced in the theory part of this book. As mentioned above, we will use the Vatn analysis (Vatn 2005) as the starting point.

The objective of the analysis is to present a risk picture with respect to third parties, that is, the residents of Frøystad, children and the staff at the kindergarten, including the parents of children attending the kindergarten. The analysis builds on

- system knowledge concerning the design and operation of the NOKAS facility;

- relevant statistical material related to robberies;

- discussions with the NOKAS personnel, the police and third parties;

- statements and considerations from experts and

- statements and considerations from third parties.

The work is carried out by a group of risk analysts, supported by experts in the areas of risk perception and communication.

The analysis will be followed up politically. Is the safety level acceptable? What type of measures are required to reach an acceptable level of safety?

10.1.2   Selection of analysis method

The objective of the analysis is to present a risk picture, and this involves a description that covers (A, C, P, K) using the terminology introduced in Chapter 2. There may be differing views on the important issues, and this will be reflected by the risk description.

A model-based risk analysis is used in this case. The risk is judged to be relatively large, and in order to give the politicians a solid basis for their decisions, a thorough and detailed analysis that provides an informed picture of the risk is required.

There is significant uncertainty associated with how many robberies we will experience in the future and the form that these will take. The world is changing, and it is likely that large changes will take place in how robberies occur over the coming years. As a result, it is important to bring forward the uncertainties and not just present a risk picture using probabilities. Based on the identified initiating events (hazards/threats), the analysis will look at causes and consequences and, in this way, establish a set of scenarios. In addition, an important task is to identify the most important risk-influencing factors.

For the assigned probabilities, sensitivity analysis must be carried out, showing how the numerical values depend on the assumptions made.

The results of the risk analysis are assessed in relation to a set of principles, such as comparison with other activities, the cautionary principle and ALARP, in order to provide a basis for judging whether the risk is acceptable or not. The final conclusion could be different depending on how much weight the politicians give to the various principles.

10.2   Risk analysis

10.2.1   Identification of hazards and threats

The following list of main hazard/threat scenarios were identified:

1. robbery of a money conveyance without intention to enter the cash depot;

2. hijacking a money conveyance with the purpose of getting inside the NOKAS facility;

3. use of explosives to gain entry into the NOKAS facility;

4. use of hostages to gain entry into the NOKAS facility;

5. use of 'insiders' to gain entry into the NOKAS facility;

6. robbery of a large money conveyance and

7. others

This list was drawn up after examination of earlier studies of this type, historical events and special threat identification sessions run by the analysis team. The seventh category, 'others,' was added, because it is of course conceivable that robberies in the future may not occur in any of the ways described by the scenarios 1–6. Although we deem this as not very likely, it must still be addressed. It is a part of the risk picture (uncertainty picture) that also needs to be included. If we overlook a potential threat, then the associated risk is not taken into account in the results.

10.2.2   Cause analysis

Most robberies of large cash holdings are aimed at money conveyances. The immediate objective of such robberies is to seize the money inside the vehicle by force. In Norway, there has not been a systematic increase in the number of such robberies, but Sweden has experienced a tripling in the past 7 years.

On average, there have been six robberies or attempted robberies of money conveyances per year in Norway in the past 5 years. The number of 'destinations' (NOKAS facilities) is calculated to be 20. A history-based probability that an attempt will be made to rob a money conveyance on its way to/from the NOKAS facility at Frøystad is then $6/20 = 0.30$, that is, 30% per year. Historically, few robberies have taken place close to the destination or in the vicinity of where the money conveyance picks up the cash, because of more safety precautions there than on the 'highway.'

One can, of course, discuss the reference numbers used here. Which year should be used as the starting point? Why the past 5 years? Why not the past 10 years or the past 3 years? If, rather than using the number of depots (NOKASs) as a basis, one looks at the number of money conveyances, the number of cash depots and so on, then the exposure level would indicate that the Gausel facility represents less than the assumption of 1 in 20 used above.

Some would argue that the future will witness more robberies where force will be used. The arguments are given as follows:

- Organised crime is a problem that is on increase both in Norway and elsewhere in Europe.

- Norway is experiencing that certain criminal groups, from certain countries, are establishing themselves in the country.

- The extension of the European Union to the east, and the opening up of borders in the Schengen Agreement, promises a 'free movement of crime'.

- Recent events have indicated an increase in the use of force in robberies and attempted robberies.

There are, however, many arguments supporting the statement that the number of robberies will decrease:

- Systematic safety and security work is being undertaken by the industry to counteract the conditions noted above.

- In particular, the facility at Gausel is characterised by an entirely different standard of safety/security than those facilities that have been robbed in recent years.

- It is Norwegian currency that is exposed here, and this currency is more difficult to dispose of than, for example, euros.

- From the available statistics, we do not see any negative developments, rather we see a slight trend for the better.

The number of robbery occurrences is an observable quantity that can be used as a risk indicator. A sharp change in the number of such occurrences would provide a basis for concluding that the risk has changed correspondingly. This argument is, however, built on a 'reactive' way of thinking – we first observe the event and then take action. The main point of a risk assessment is, of course, to be proactive, so that decisions can be made before serious events occur.

Based on historical figures, a prediction can be made that one event will occur over the next 3 years. However, the uncertainties are considerable. What will be the nature of the robbery? If such an event should take place, is there reason to believe that this will affect the rate of attacks or the attack approach? Yes, it may absolutely do so, as shown by the 2004 robbery in Stavanger, when a police officer was killed.

Depending on the conditions and the assumptions made, the analysis group will arrive at different probabilities for an attack. Some examples are

- the use of historical data as mentioned earlier: 30%;

- use of a larger data set for money conveyances (not only depots): 5%;

- strong growth in aggravated robbery groups: 50% and

- the robbery milieu is keeping a lower profile following the 2004 robbery: 10%.

However, it is not a major point whether one should use 30%, 10%, 50% or some other percentage. There exists a threat that the NOKAS facility will be exposed to such an event over the coming years, and the figures above give a picture of the risk level. The analysis group uses 10% as its basis value.

The analysis group also uses a 90% prediction interval to express uncertainty levels. Let X represent the number of events over the next 10 years and let K be the background knowledge. A 90% prediction interval is then given as $[a, b]$ for a and b such that

$$P(a \leq X \leq b|K) = 0.90.$$

The analysis group arrives at an interval of $[0, 2]$. It is not very probable that more than two events should occur in the period considered, but we cannot disregard this possibility in the event that we should see a strong increase in robberies.

Until now, we have looked at a total probability for a robbery attempt corresponding to the various threat scenarios (1–6). Each of these threat scenarios will be analysed and the uncertainties will be described and discussed. Let us look at one example, threat scenario 4: 'using hostages to gain entry into the NOKAS facility.'

One can envisage a variety of situations where hostages are taken. In Norway, there is one example of third parties being taken hostage in connection with a robbery. In this case, the hostages were taken soon after the robbery and at a different location from where the robbery occurred. This incident took place more than 10 years ago. Examining the number of robberies of money conveyances, banks and post offices, the historical fraction of hostage taking after a robbery is less than 1%, assuming that a robbery has indeed occurred.

In 2004, however, there was a hostage situation in Northern Ireland (Vatn 2005):

> It wasn't until around midnight on Monday, six hours after thieves had robbed the Northern Banks head office in the centre of Belfast, that the police obtained a report on the robbery. By then, the robbers had long since disappeared, with proceeds of between British £20 and 30 million. On Sunday, the bank robbers took as hostages family members of the two bank managers, and held them in their own homes. Under threat that the hostages would be harmed, the robbers forced the two executives to go to work as usual. The two were at work all day Monday. None of the other staff noticed anything unusual with the two. When the bank closed for the day on Monday, the two remained, and the robbers gained entrance into the bank.

In this scenario, the families of the employees were taken as hostages. Threats were made against the bank staff, who then 'opened the doors' for the robbers without anybody else knowing what was afoot. The fact that the employees or their families can be threatened in this way is therefore highly realistic. One can also envisage neighbours or persons at the kindergarten being taken as hostages.

Those who are taken as hostages, and their families, will no doubt become very negatively affected from such an event. At the outset, the most likely possibility is that persons who have ties to NOKAS will be taken as hostages, as opposed to neighbours or others in the vicinity. Historically, if one omits those persons directly servicing the money conveyances (drivers or reception staff), there are few events where persons are taken as hostages in order to enable robbers to gain money by force. But such reasoning does not take into account the fact that 'surprises' can happen. We must expect that if thieves intend to rob NOKAS, then they will search for new methods, and various extortion methods may become relevant.

The extent to which hostages will be seriously injured or killed depends on the evolution of the situation. The analysis group does not have access to relevant statistics but views the probability as being relatively large. We are talking here about armed robberies. A probability of 10% is assigned.

10.2.3   Consequence analysis

Starting from the initiating events, traditional event tree analyses were carried out. An example is shown in Figure 10.1, based on the threat: 'attack on money conveyance upon arrival at, or in the vicinity of, the NOKAS facility, with the objective of seizing by force the money contained in the money conveyance.' The different branches in the event tree require separate analysis. Here, we choose to look at the branches, 'hostages taken' and 'shooting occurs while fleeing the scene,' and our focus is on third parties.

Hostages taken

If an attack is carried out, many types of stressful situations involving shooting could arise, and hostages may be taken. Note that this scenario is not the same as threat scenario 4, which relates to the planned taking of hostages to enter the facility.

A relatively high probability is given for the use of hostages and for possible injuries and deaths during such stressful situations: P(hostage taking | stressful situation) = 0.2, P(fatalities | hostage taking, stressful situation) = 0.2, and P(injuries | hostage taking, stressful situation) = 0.5.

Shooting occurs while fleeing the scene

While robbers are fleeing the scene, shooting may occur. A probability of 10% is assigned for such an event given that the two first branch events have not occurred. The probability is rather low because of the safety philosophy of the police. This policy implies that third parties are not to be put in danger in order to arrest criminals. This means that if a robbery comes about, and the police are notified, then they will

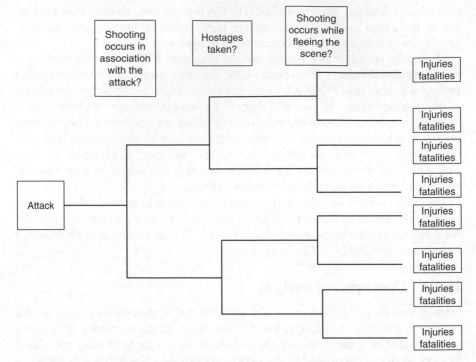

Figure 10.1   Event tree for the threat attack.

first conduct a reconnaissance of the area. Prior to the police potentially taking an action, the area will be evacuated. Regarding possible car chases, a stronger competence level is required for the police than for the fire department and ambulance personnel. Furthermore, there has been a shift from not 'giving up on a car chase' to a policy of giving up on the car chase as soon as it is judged that the chase represents a danger for third parties or for those being chased (or the police itself). On 'paper,' there is therefore no hazard associated with either gunfire or car chases when the police is involved. However, one cannot exclude conflict situations. Such situations can arise from misjudgement of the situation by the police, or by them not handling the situation by the book.

If one or both of the previous branch events have occurred, significantly higher probabilities are assigned. If the police enter a situation where a critical state has already set in (e.g. NOKAS staff or a third party is in immediate danger), it is much more likely that shooting will occur while fleeing the scene.

In case of such a scenario, it is likely that persons in the escape route could be injured or killed. One may expect groups of children and adults in the escape area. During an escape, one or more of these persons may be injured or killed. The analysis group assigns a probability of 5% that someone will be killed under such a situation and 25% that someone will be injured. There are no available statistics concerning the number of persons killed and injured for this type of escape situations. It is, however, very rare that third persons are killed in an escape situation with the police involved. On the other hand, it is not unusual for those being pursued to be injured or killed.

Barriers

In the NOKAS facility, there are many barriers to prevent attacks and to limit the losses in the event of an attack:

- There is a reinforced perimeter with installed alarms on windows, doors and vehicular entry/exit locks.

- Money conveyance vehicles must enter through the vehicular locks (vehicle reception room), and dedicated control processes are in place to allow entry of these vehicles.

- Within the outer perimeter, there is another perimeter with personnel entry locks into the internal reception room (valuables zone). Only one person can enter at a time, and timed barriers are installed to deter many persons from entering within a short time period.

- Between the vehicular room and the reception room (valuables zone), there is only one lock for valuables alone, that is, neither people nor vehicles can move between the vehicle room and the reception room.

- The vault itself is located inside the valuables zone.

- To control taking money out of the vault, the doors to the vault are equipped with time-delay locks.

- There are systems in place to destroy/secure the money in a robbery situation.

We cannot discuss these conditions in any more detail here.

Based on these analyses, one can calculate probabilities for the two chosen consequence categories: injured and killed (see below).

10.3   Risk picture

Based on the analysis in the preceding section, a risk picture is established. It contains the usual elements (A, C, P, K).

A series of threats (initiating events) have been identified and the consequences analysed. On this basis, a list of possible scenarios have emerged. Furthermore, important factors influencing the initiating events and consequences are discussed. Quantitative analyses are carried out to determine how likely the different events and scenarios are. The analyses yield the following probabilities (for a period of one year):

- A probability of 10% for an attack associated with the NOKAS facility

- A probability of 0.01% that a third person will be seriously injured or killed as a result of a NOKAS-related attack.

There are, in particular, two uncertainty aspects that apply:

- Possible trends within the robbery environment

- The scenario development in the case of an attack.

Depending on the assumptions made with respect to these aspects, one can arrive at different probability figures. Our assumptions are drawn from the analysis above. A particularly important point is the manner in which a possible attack will take place. A possible scenario is that an attack will occur in an innovative, surprising and brutal way. The use of hostages is a clear possibility during such an attack, and the result could easily be injuries and fatalities. If we assume a strong increase in the aggravated robbery environment, we will arrive at a probability of 0.1% for a third person being seriously injured or killed as a result of a NOKAS-related attack.

The aforementioned figures relate to events where at least one person is seriously injured or killed. If we wish to calculate individual risk, then we must focus on the event in which one specific person is seriously injured or killed. Given that there are approximately 100 persons who are exposed, the aforementioned figures must be divided by 100.

An event can result in a number of injuries and fatalities. The drama inherent in an attack suggests that each and every attack discussed above must be viewed as a major accident. Even if only one person is injured or killed, the character of the event is violent and could lead to considerable ripple effects, both for those in the vicinity of the facility and for the community as a whole. The psychological strain can be strong and can lead to long-term suffering and trauma.

Using such arguments, we arrive at a probability of 0.1–1% for a major accident, depending on the assumptions made.

In order to judge the level of risk, we draw attention to some reference values:

- The number of people killed in accidents in Norway in recent years has been, on average, approximately 1700 per year. This means that an 'average person' has a probability at $4 \cdot 10^{-4}$ of being killed in an accident over the course of 1 year. Of these accidents, 20% take place in a residence or in a residential area, while 20% result from traffic accidents.

- It is common to require a probability of death of a third person associated with exposure from an industrial plant to be less than 10^{-5} (for 1 year).

- It is usual to require a probability for a 'major accident' to be less than 10^{-4} (for 1 year).

- There are very few accidents where children are killed during the time they are attending a kindergarten. Statistics on fatalities in kindergartens and in playgrounds show 0.7 fatalities per year. This corresponds to a yearly probability of $4 \cdot 10^{-6}$ that a child will be killed in an accident in a kindergarten or at a playground (the statistics do not distinguish between playgrounds and kindergartens).

- The 'average, historical probability' of being killed in a robbery, or in an assault is 10^{-5} per year.

- The German MEM (Minimum Endogenous Mortality) principle refers to a basic risk and makes a point that any new activity must not produce an additional risk that is significant compared to the basic risk. The MEM principle means that an additional risk is unacceptable if it represents a risk for individual persons that is greater than 10^{-5} per year.

- There is usually a lower acceptance for risk concerning children than for adults.

- The risk we accept is linked to the benefits we gain from the activity. Considerable risk is accepted for driving a car, as we derive a great benefit from this activity. The benefit for the residents of Frøystad from the NOKAS facility, however, is small.

From the analysis figures, and comparison of these with the reference values, in particular, the MEM principle, the individual risk does not come out too badly. However, if we consider a robbery to be a major accident, the assessment would be different. In such a case, the figures would be relatively high.

There is uncertainty associated with whether we will experience an attack linked to the NOKAS facility in the future and what the course of events will be if an attack should actually occur. This fact calls for the application of the cautionary principle. This principle states that if one is faced with a significant risk, measures must be put into effect to avoid or reduce this risk (refer Section 1.2.1). The ALARP principle is an example of how this principle can be implemented in practice. ALARP involves a reversed burden of proof. A safety measure should be implemented unless the disadvantages (including costs) are not disproportionate to the benefits gained.

10.4   Risk-reducing measures

Various measures are suggested, including

- relocation of the NOKAS facility;
- relocation of the kindergarten;

- the erection of a wall between the NOKAS facility and the kindergarten;

- covering the NOKAS facility with panels and

- review of the emergency preparedness procedures for the kindergarten.

We will take a closer look at two of these measures in the following sections:

10.4.1   Relocation of the NOKAS facility

The measure that obviously has the greatest risk-reducing effect for third parties is to relocate the NOKAS facility. If the facility is relocated to an area that is zoned exclusively for commercial activity, using an appropriate location plan, there will be few persons (third parties) exposed compared to the threat scenarios identified earlier. The analysis group's assessment is that the risk then would be practically eliminated. The cost of relocating the NOKAS facility is calculated to be 50 million kroner (NOK) (about €6 million). For a period of 30 years, the expected number of saved lives will be 0.03 (calculated on the basis of 0.001 per year), and this means that the cost per expected number of lives saved will be $50/0.03 = 1700$ (million NOK).

This is a very high number, and normally one would conclude that the cost is disproportionate compared to the benefits gained.

The argument here, however, is a traditional cost-benefit analysis, and as discussed in Section 3.1, this approach is not very suitable for expressing the benefits of the safety measure. The risk reduction is greater than the changes in the computed expected value, as argued in the previous section. How much is it worth to remove this risk? The question is about assigning weights to various concerns, including risk, and this issue is the responsibility of the politicians. It is clear that significant emphasis must be given to the cautionary principle if one is to be able to justify this measure.

10.4.2   Erection of a wall

If a wall is built between the kindergarten and the NOKAS facility, the risk is judged to be significantly reduced. Such a wall is assumed to provide a good effect, since gunfire situations represent a significant contribution to the overall risk. Such a wall may also have a positive effect in relation to escape situations. The total risk reduction obtained by erecting such a wall is calculated to be 30%. The cost of erecting such a wall is 500,000 NOK. This gives the following cost-benefit ratio: $0.5/0.01 = 50$ (million NOK).

This measure is also relatively expensive from this perspective, but one is now closer to values normally used to justify safety investments. But as for the first measure, a broader evaluation process must take place to judge the appropriateness of the measure.

Various arguments have been presented from the residents in connection with such a measure. Some have expressed their interest in such a wall provided it is aesthetically constructed. Others have pointed out that erection of such a wall would show that NOKAS constitutes a real threat and that it will serve to intensify the existing negative risk perception.

10.5   Management review and judgement. Decision

The decision that the politicians make is dependent on how they weigh the different concerns. The analysis has presented a risk picture and various measures are assessed. The limitations and the assumptions on which these are built are presented as a part of this picture and these assessments. Together, these provide a good basis for decision-making.

10.6   Discussion

Our analysis and the use we make of it differ from that in Vatn (2005) in several ways, the most important being:

- The risk description is different. We place a stronger emphasis on the uncertainty dimension, in addition to the probabilities.

- We expand the basis for judging about acceptance of the risk by considering an event of type 1–6 in Section 10.2.1 as a major accident.

- We stress that traditional cost-benefit analyses do not properly reflect risk and, as a result, are not well suited to show the appropriateness of safety measures.

When viewed as a whole, our analysis provides a somewhat more informative and reflective perspective than that of Vatn (2005). For decision-makers, this is not necessarily seen as an advantage, but we believe that it is important. It provides enhanced clarity on what is in the domain of safety professionals and what is the responsibility of politicians.

In the analysis, we did not report on or discuss the risk perception of the neighbours and the staff at the kindergarten. Risk perception contains a cognitive analysis and evaluation of the risk, but it also contains emotional components such as fear, worry and anxiety. Separate processes were carried out in order to examine and discuss the risk perception for these groups. We do not, however, go into these processes in any further detail here.

Reflection

To what extent do the politicians wish a more informative and reflective perspective, such as the one that we recommend?

There will clearly be different opinions on such a perspective among our politicians. Some will be sceptical because they must do more independent evaluations and thus accept greater responsibility. The administration and the bureaucracy will not provide as clear recommendations as one otherwise is often accustomed to receive from them. Others will say that this is the correct path.

11

Risk analysis process for municipalities

This chapter presents a risk analysis process for municipalities. The presentation is partly based on Wiencke et al. (2007).

11.1 Planning

11.1.1 Problem definition

The objective of this analysis is to identify risk critical events in a region consisting of several municipalities and to identify the events that are design-critical for the emergency preparedness at the regional level. These events will be followed up in a preparedness analysis. The goal is not to quantify the risk level within the region, but rather, to rank the events in order to select those that are design-critical for the emergency preparedness task. Minor events that are dealt with on a daily basis by the municipal and regional stakeholders are not covered by the analysis. The analysis involves the municipalities and the region in normal operation for all times of the year. Conditions that arise in states of emergency and war are not included in the analysis.

The focus of the analysis is on safety for persons, primarily against events that can cause a large number of fatalities or injuries and that thereby will place a major demand on the preparedness resources within the municipalities and in the region. In addition, events that could affect several consequence dimensions are highlighted, such as personal safety, the external environment and cultural heritage (e.g. fires in very old buildings).

Risk Analysis, Second Edition. Terje Aven.
© 2015 John Wiley & Sons, Ltd. Published 2015 by John Wiley & Sons, Ltd.

11.1.2   Selection of analysis method

Based on the objective of the risk analysis, the decision was made to carry out a standard risk analysis. The method is described in the section that follows.

In order to be able to identify events and to rank them, it is necessary to establish an analysis principle or procedure. The following procedure was selected in this analysis.

First, we select some events from a long list of undesirable events, based on two criteria:

- Events in which expected losses are high, from a personal safety point of view.

- Events in which there are considerable uncertainties associated with the outcome of the events, for example, as a result of large uncertainties in underlying phenomena and processes.

Expected loss for an event is determined by the product of frequency and consequence, where consequence is interpreted as the expected consequence should the event occur. This value is set on the basis of an analysis of historical data at a high level and local knowledge regarding the event.

Expected loss alone, however, is not enough to describe the risk. Consider the following example.

Example

If driving one's car off the road occurs 10 times per year, each occurrence with an average of 0.5 fatalities, then the associated expected loss (expected number of fatalities in the course of a year) will be $0.5 \cdot 10 = 5$ persons per year. If driving a bus off the road occurs every other year with an average of 10 fatalities, then the expected number of fatalities in the course of a year will also be 5 persons. The expected loss per year is the same, but the risk picture is completely different and would place very different demands on the handling of such events. Figure 11.1 shows an example of a probability distribution associated with the consequences of a bus accident. The figure shows that, most likely, the event will result in severe injuries, but the event can yield a spectrum of outcomes ranging from insignificant consequences to many fatalities.

Emergency preparedness analyses will be carried out for those events that result in high expected losses, as well as the events characterised by large uncertainties.

11.2   Risk assessment

11.2.1   Hazard and threat identification

The aim of this activity is to determine a list of critical threats and hazards. The activity is carried out via the following sub-activities:

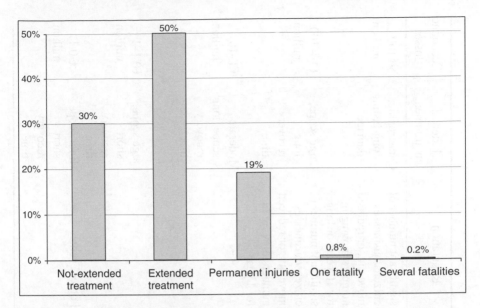

Figure 11.1   Probability distribution associated with the consequences of a bus accident.

- Establish a preliminary event list based on earlier analyses carried out within and outside the region.

- Establish an event hierarchy in order to structure the events and the list. Grouping is done in such a way that the categories, to the greatest possible extent, conform to the Police's Rescue Services plan. The following structure is used:

  - main categories, for example, fire;

  - subcategories, for example, fire at accommodation places;

  - specific scenarios, for example, fire in hotels.

- Review of the list in a regional meeting with representatives from the relevant municipalities and regional stakeholders, such as power companies, water processing plants and transport companies (rail and highway).

- Review of the list in meetings with representatives from the various municipalities.

The result of the process was a list with more than 300 events, arranged into 20 major categories with their subcategories.

Table 11.1 Consequence categories.

		Injuries	Important community functions	Reputation	External environment	Economic losses
5	Catastrophic	>10 fatalities and/or >10 hospitalised	Loss of important community functions for >10,000 persons for >3 days	A significant number of citizens/businesses move out, or reduced numbers moving in for 10 years or longer	Catastrophic, long-lasting damage	>€100 million
4	Very severe	3–10 fatalities and/or 5–10 hospitalised	Loss of important community functions for 1000–9999 persons for >3 days	A significant number of citizens/businesses move out, or reduced numbers moving in for 1 year	Large scope, long recovery time	€10–100 million
3	Severe	1–2 fatalities or 3–5 persons hospitalised	Loss of important community functions for 100–999 persons for >3 days, or for >1000 persons for up to 24 h	–	Moderate scope, long recovery time	€1–10 million
2	Less severe	1–2 persons hospitalised	Loss of important community functions for 10–99 persons for up to 24 h	–	Large scope, short recovery time	€0.1–1 million
1	Not severe	Injuries that can be treated by primary health care	Loss of important community functions for 1–9 persons for up to 24 h	All other events	Minor scope, short recovery time	<€0.1 million

Table 11.2   Categories of frequency/probability.

Frequency/probability category	Frequency prediction	Probability
5	Once per 1–10 years	0.1 or larger
4	Once per 10–100 years	0.1–0.01
3	Once per 100–1000 years	0.01–0.001
2	Once per 1000–10,000 years	0.001–0.0001
1	<once per 10,000 years	<0.0001

Table 11.3   Main categories of events.

1	Fire in special fire sites	12	Criminal acts
2	Explosion	13	Failure of infrastructure – Electricity
3	Railroad accident	14	Failure of infrastructure – Water
4	Airline accidents	15	Failure of infrastructure – Sewage
5	Accidents at sea	16	Failure of infrastructure – Renovation
6	Road traffic (accidents)	17	Failure of infrastructure – Transport network
7	Health decline – persons	18	Failure of infrastructure – ICT
8	Health decline – pets	19	Administrative failure (community)
9	Health decline – farmed animals	20	Nuclear accidents
10	Health decline – wild animals	21	Spill of hazardous goods/ contamination
11	Evacuation	22	Natural disasters

11.2.2   Cause and consequence analysis. Risk picture

The starting point of the analysis was the overall frequency figure for the various events on a national or regional level, obtained from the Directorate for Civil Protection and Emergency Planning, and various research projects, among others. The figures are discussed and adjusted on the basis of knowledge about the region brought out in meetings with the municipalities and regional stakeholders. Viewed in relation to the objective of this analysis – to select the events that should be assessed further in a preparedness analysis – this procedure was deemed to be satisfactory.

The events assessed are classified into frequency and consequence classes as shown in Tables 11.1–11.3 and Figure 11.2. The events are positioned in relation to the expected losses in terms of life and health. Events with large uncertainties are highlighted. The numbers assigned to the events in the matrix correspond to those of the

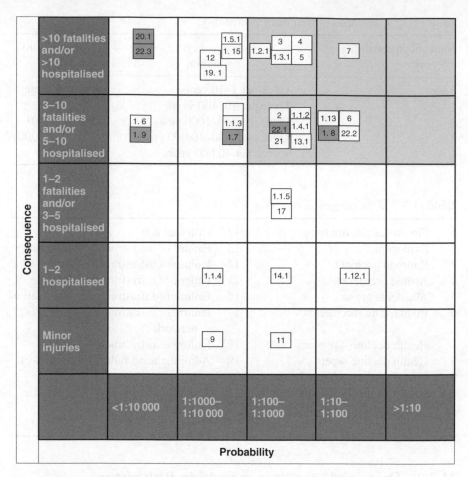

Figure 11.2   Risk matrix based on expected loss. Events with large uncertainty with respect to outcome are highlighted (grey).

main categories in Table 11.3, that is, an event marked 1.5.1 or 1.2.1 is an event in category 1, "fire in special fire sites".

11.3   Risk treatment

Table 11.4 shows the list of selected events. High expected losses are defined here as events that have occurrence probability higher than 0.001 (1:1000 years) in the region and with consequences above 2 fatalities and 5–10 persons hospitalised.

Table 11.4   Selected events.

Number	High expected losses	Large uncertainties (poor knowledge base)	Defined hazard and accident events
1.1.2	X		Fire – institution – health-care institutions
1.2.1	X		Fire – accommodation places – hotels
1.3.1	X		Fire – sports arenas and grandstand facilities
1.4.1	X	X	Fire – underground facilities – road tunnels
1.7		X	Fire – objects covered by permits in accordance with regulations
1.8	X	X	Fire – sites where the fire could constitute a serious threat to the environment
1.9		X	Fire – important cultural and historical buildings and sites
1.13	X		Fire – industrial fires
2	X		Explosions
3	X		Railway accidents
4	X		Airline accidents
5	X		Accidents at sea
6	X		Road traffic accidents
7	X		(Decline) health – persons
13.1	X		Failure of infrastructure–electricity (long duration)
20.1		X	Nuclear accidents – reactor vessel
21	X		Spill of hazardous goods/contamination
22.1	X	X	Natural disasters – storms/hurricanes
22.2	X		Natural disasters – landslide/avalanches – mud-slides
22.3		X	Natural disasters – tsunamis

The selected events are assessed in more detail and processed further in a preparedness analysis.

For a more recent study of this type, see Flage et al. (2014).

12

Risk analysis process for the entire enterprise

An enterprise performs a risk analysis to describe risk related to all of its activities. The analysis provides a basis for supporting decisions on investments and risk-reducing measures.

12.1 Planning

12.1.1 Problem definition

The risk picture to be established covers all aspects of (A, C, P, K), using the notation introduced in Chapter 2. In order to obtain a structure for the risk picture, a distinction is made between various types of risk:

- Financial and commercial risk, including risk related to foreign exchange rates, interest rate, credit and prices.

- Operational risk, which includes risk associated with the unavailability of the production system and ICT security.

- Health, environment and safety (HES).

- Other risks, including risk associated with political decisions and reputation.

Risk Analysis, Second Edition. Terje Aven.
© 2015 John Wiley & Sons, Ltd. Published 2015 by John Wiley & Sons, Ltd.

Furthermore, a distinction is made among the various parties involved:

- The enterprise
- Important partners, for example, suppliers, banks and financial services
- Others, for example, the regulators and public opinion.

The main perspective for the risk analysis is the enterprise and its owners.

For the different types of risk, a series of more specific risk analyses are conducted, based on various data sources. For example, comprehensive statistics are available on the prices of the various products, accident events and so on.

12.1.2 Selection of analysis method

The assessment builds on a series of risk assessments carried out for the various types of risks. These risk analyses are of different types: model-based, standard and simplified.

12.2 Risk analysis

Let us look into some of the specific risk analyses conducted, for price, operational risk, HES and reputation.

12.2.1 Price risk

Table 12.1 and Figure 12.1 show the prices for two products manufactured by the enterprise, product 1 and product 2, during the past 12 months.

Based on these figures, the average prices and the empirical standard deviations can be calculated; see Table 12.2.

The empirical standard deviation S is calculated as the square root of the empirical variance:

$$S^2 = \sum_{i=1}^{n} \frac{(X_i - M)^2}{n},$$

where X_i is the price for month i, M is the mean value and n is the number of observations (in this case 12). It is also common to refer to the spread (variance) as the volatility.

Table 12.1   Prices for Two Products Per Month.

Month product	1	2	3	4	5	6	7	8	9	10	11	12
1	10	11	13	12	13	12	14	13	14	15	17	17
2	12	11	12	14	14	14	16	15	16	13	12	13

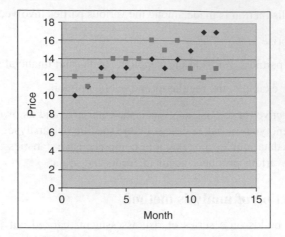

Figure 12.1   Prices for two products per month.

Table 12.2   Means and Empirical Standard Deviations.

Product	Average price (M)	Empirical standard deviation (S)
1	13.42	2.06
2	13.50	1.56

We see that the average price of the two products is about the same, but the standard deviation and the variance are significantly larger for product 1. It seems that the price for product 1 is increasing.

Let us now look at the risk. What is the risk associated with prices? The above figures do not show the risk, only the historical figures. We can use these figures to say something about the future and risk.

If we base our analysis on the figures for predictions and uncertainty assessments, we arrive at the following risk picture:

Let $X(1)$ and $X(2)$ be the prices for the two products during the next month. Then, our prediction for the Xs is provided by

$$X(1)^* = EX(1) = 13.4$$

$$X(2)^* = EX(2) = 13.5.$$

Furthermore, 90% prediction intervals are provided by

$$X(1) : [11, 17]$$

$$X(2) : [12, 16],$$

as at least 90% of the observations are within these intervals. If we use a normal distribution to express the probability, with expectation and variance equal to the empirical values, then we obtain the following 90% prediction intervals:

$$X(1) : [10.0, 16.8]$$

$$X(2) : [10.9, 16.1].$$

We have used that $(X - M)/S$ is normally distributed with expectation 0 and variance 1. Let us look at the calculations for the first interval, $X(1) : [10.0, 16.8]$. Since $(X - M)/S$ is normally distributed with expectation 0 and standard deviation 1, we obtain

$$P\left(-c \leq \frac{(X - M)}{S} \leq c\right) = 0.90,$$

where $c = 1.645$. We obtain the quantile c from normal distribution tables. This yields

$$P(M - cS \leq X \leq M + cS) = 0.90,$$

and the interval $[M - cS, M + cS] = [10.0, 16.8]$ follows.

We see that the prediction intervals using the normal distribution are approximately equal to those first established.

But, can we rely on these predictions? If there is a trend in price levels for product 1, it would be more reasonable to predict a price level of about 18 and not 13.4. If we use the same variance as above, we arrive at a prediction interval of [14, 22]. With hindsight, we can show which one is the best prediction, but the analysis makes it clear that a simple transformation of the historical figures can lead to poor predictions.

By attempting to understand the data, by assuming a trend and carrying out a regression analysis (see Aven (2012d)), we may be able to improve the predictions. But we may also end up with 'over-interpreting' the data in the sense that we look for all sorts of explanations for why the historical figures are as they are. Perhaps prices are rising; perhaps the trend arrow will be reversed next month. We can analyse possible underlying conditions that can affect prices, but it is not easy to reflect what the important factors are and what is 'noise' or arbitrariness.

An analysis based on the historical numbers could easily become too narrow and imply that extreme outcomes are ignored. Surprises occur from time to time, and suddenly an event could occur that dramatically changes the development, with the consequence that the prices jump up or down. In a risk analysis such events should be identified. However, the problem is that we do not always have the knowledge and insights to be able to identify such events, because they are surprising relative to our beliefs and knowledge (Taleb (2007), Aven and Krohn (2014)).

As a result, it is important to see the analysis in a larger context, where its constraints and boundaries are taken into account.

Finally, we make a comment on the correlation between the two product prices. It is to be expected, perhaps, that there would be a correspondence between the prices of the two products: high prices for one product generally show high values for the other product, and correspondingly so for low values. The empirical correlation coefficient (r) can be used to express this correspondence. The formula used is:

$$r = \sum_i \frac{(X_i(1) - M_1)(X_i(2) - M_2)}{[n \cdot S(1)S(2)]}.$$

In this case, r is equal to 0.12. The correlation is thus relatively small. An r equal to zero corresponds to no correlation and an r equal to 1 and -1 corresponds to 'perfect' correlation, respectively, in the same direction and in the opposite direction. The reader is referred to textbooks in statistics.

12.2.2   Operational risk

This risk covers production losses as analysed in Chapter 9. Furthermore, intentional acts and security issues are included, for example, a failure in the ICT system as a result of hacking. Let us take a closer look at the last mentioned type of events. A risk analysis of such events begins by identifying the initiating events (the threats), taken from experience from earlier analyses, statistics and activities and methods such as Failure Modes and Effects Analysis (FMEA) and Hazard and Operability study (HAZOP). The threat identification is closely related to the cause analysis, in that actual threats quickly lead to discussion of scenarios, causes, uncertainties and probabilities.

The cause analysis typically comprises the following steps:

- Information gathering
- Identification of scenarios
- Probability assignments
- Uncertainty/knowledge assessments.

Based on the identified events, analyses can be carried out by using fault trees, event trees and Bayesian networks. Such analyses provide a set of possible scenarios that can lead to the initiating events. These analyses are aimed at exposing the vulnerabilities of the system with regard to potential attacks.

The next part of the analysis will be an analysis of the attacker's resources and may cover aspects such as

- resources needed to carry out the attack;
- possible attackers;
- attackers' motivation, competence, resource base and capabilities in carrying out the attack and
- knowledge and access to the system to be attacked.

In addition, we examine factors that may affect the success of potential attackers, the system's function and the barriers that are in place to prevent the attack and limit damaging effects. Examples of such performance- influencing factors are intelligence and surveillance.

Next, the analysis addresses issues such as:

- How likely is it that an attack as described will be carried out over a given period of time?

- Are there large uncertainties associated with underlying phenomena and processes?

The analyst may, for example, assign a probability of 1% that an event will happen given a set of background conditions. This probability may be assigned directly or may be based on more detailed analyses, for example, fault trees, as described earlier.

The *consequence analysis* consists of steps corresponding to those of the cause analysis. The event tree analysis would normally be an important part of the consequence analysis. The event tree analysis results in a set of possible scenarios with specified loss categories. When event trees have been developed, uncertainty assessments can be made and probabilities assigned. The vulnerability of the system, should an initiating event occur, is analysed as a part of the consequence analysis.

The event tree analysis must be supplemented with more specific analysis of system vulnerability, which could bring out the characteristic features of the system. An example of such an analysis is presented by Anton et al. (2003). This analysis is based on the identification of vulnerabilities by using a checklist covering an extensive taxonomy associated with physical, cyber, human/organisational and infrastructural objects and covers aspects such as

- Design/architecture
  - singularity – uniqueness, centrality and homogeneity
  - separability
  - logic/implementation errors – fallibility
  - design sensitivity – fragility, limits and finiteness
  - unrecoverability.

- Behavioural
  - behavioural sensitivity/fragility
  - malevolence
  - rigidity
  - malleability
  - gullibility – deceivability, naiveté
  - complacency
  - corruptibility – controllability.

- General
  - accessible – detectable, identifiable, transparent and interceptable
  - hard to manage or control
  - self-unawareness and unpredictability
  - predictability.

With the help of a systematic examination of these attributes, vulnerabilities that are not obvious can be identified. Note that this vulnerability analysis is also relevant for the cause analysis above. Vulnerability can be identified for different initiating events at various steps in the scenario.

Various consequence categories can be defined. For information systems, it is common to use attributes such as confidentiality, integrity and availability (Dondossola et al. 2004).

The analysis will then look at uncertainties and probabilities as was done in the cause analysis. The analysts can, for example, arrive at a probability of 30% for a specific consequence given the initiating event and the associated background knowledge.

The above analysis can be summarised in a standard risk matrix, with the dimensions probability and expected consequence. In addition, the uncertainty associated with the underlying phenomena (strength of knowledge) must be discussed. A specific method is outlined in Section 12.2.4.

In particular, one could be concerned about the risk associated with large losses. What would it take for the loss to become greater than, for example, €d million? How likely is that such an event will occur? What factors affect this likelihood? Often, focus is placed on distribution quantiles, for example, the 95% quantile (v), defined in such a way that the probability of a loss exceeding v, is 5%, i.e. $P(loss > v) = 0.05$. It is common to refer to this quantile as the VaR, or Value-at-Risk, as mentioned in Section 2.3.1.

There is very little relevant data for specifying such probabilities, and the analysis described in the earlier paragraph can provide an improved basis for the quantification, but the quantitative part must still be regarded as a supplement to the qualitative assessments – the figures by themselves have limited value.

12.2.3   Health, environment and safety (HES)

HES focuses on many aspects, but here we will limit ourselves to looking at injuries caused by some chemicals in the manufacturing process. These chemicals seem to lead to health problems, but there is considerable uncertainty associated with the effect they have. There is pressure on management to reduce the use of these chemicals and to replace these with other, less hazardous, substances. The chemicals are also harmful to the external environment, and because of these concerns, it would be desirable to make a change. However, the economic motivation for using the existing chemicals is strong.

A risk assessment is carried out to describe the risk associated with the use of these chemicals. The focus is on the risk related to health and the external environment.

At an overall level, the consequences C of the chemical usage can, for example, be formulated as follows:

C = the number of persons who develop serious health problems during the course of a given period of time

where 'serious' is given a clear definition, either from a medical standpoint or based on criteria related to absence from work.

The historical figures do not provide a clear picture of how large C could be. There have been no serious problems so far, but there is a danger that the impacts arise following some years of exposure.

The historical figures from other enterprises worldwide provide only limited information, in that it is difficult to obtain completely comparable activities. Besides, experience concerning the use of these chemicals is limited, even on a world basis.

Experts on the chemicals compile all the relevant statistical information, in addition to general information on the chemicals and their effects on human beings and the environment, and then determine a probability distribution for C, as shown in Table 12.3.

The experts predict $C^* = 2$, but point out that the uncertainties are significant. Based on the existing knowledge, the event that a large number of persons can develop health problems from the use of the chemicals cannot be disregarded. There are large uncertainties associated with the outcome. It is also possible that no one gets serious health problems.

Risk assessments for the external environment are carried out in the same way. There is no indication that the use of chemicals by the enterprise has a negative effect on the external environment, in terms of how the chemicals affect animals, plants and microorganisms. Measurements confirm this, but there is still some uncertainty associated with these measurements and their ability to detect all the consequences. There is little knowledge about the effect of the chemicals in nature, especially concerning the long-term effects.

12.2.4   Reputation risk

The enterprise is concerned about events that can damage their good name and reputation and, as a result, may lead to loss of revenue, for example, from boycotts or other type of actions by various groups.

Table 12.3   The Number of Persons Who Develop
Serious Health Problems Over a Given Period of Time.

C values	0	1–5	>5
Probability (%)	50	25	25

An analysis of such potential events (*A*) is carried out. The basis is a review of historical material on what can bring about a loss of reputation. After this, a brainstorming session among key persons in the enterprise is carried out, wherein an attempt is made to identify other possible events that can result in such a consequence. Examples of such events are accusations of corruption and poor product quality. The list of events that is then generated is described by using the dimension probability (*P*) and consequence (*C*), as shown in Figure 12.2. The uncertainty factors that can produce considerable deviation relative to the expectation that is produced by the risk matrix are then reviewed; see Figure 12.3.

In a practical case, risk categories can be defined according to the following structure:

Scores expected value calculation (Figure 12.2): high, medium and low
Scores overall performance (Figure 12.3): high, medium and low.

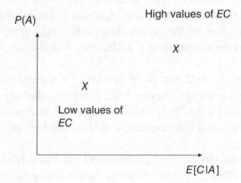

Figure 12.2   A standard risk description with components P(A) and E[C|A]. Here the X's represent specified values for two different events.

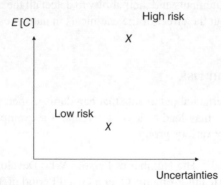

Figure 12.3   Risk description based on the components, expected consequence and uncertainty in the underlying phenomena and processes. The X's represent risk determined for two different events.

Starting from the classification based on the expected values, we may modify the classification based on the uncertainties. For example, if a system is classified as having a medium risk in relation to the expected value, we can reclassify it as high if the uncertainties in the underlying phenomena and processes are large.

In order to classify a system in terms of such a scheme, there is a need for a crude analysis. However, detailed analyses are often available, and in such cases, these will form the basis for the classification.

We have assumed that the consequences are one dimensional. In practice, we may deal with many attributes (costs, safety, etc.). In that case, descriptions as shown in Figures 12.2 and 12.3 must be established for each attribute. Summarising indices can then be defined for these attributes, for example, by summarising the scores for the various attributes.

12.3   Overall risk picture

A risk picture is presented based on the various risk types mentioned above. A simplified overview is shown in Table 12.4. The perspective is the risk picture of the enterprise, from the point of view of potential losses. It is implied, for example, that a medium high classification for price, insofar as expectation is concerned, means that the price is expected to be moderately high in the next time period to be studied. A high value is assigned if the price is expected to be low, in that our focus is on potential losses.

A certain amount of loss is expected in the production as a result of maintenance operations in the coming period.

Table 12.4   Simplified Risk Picture.

Area	Expectation $(P(A) \cdot E[C|A])$	Underlying uncertainty	Combined
Financial and commercial risk			
-Price	Medium	Medium	Medium
...			
Operational risk			
-Production	Medium	Small	Medium
-ICT	Small	Medium	Medium
HES	Medium	Large	Large
Other risks			
-Reputation	Small	Medium–large	Medium–large
...			
Total	Medium	Medium	Medium

High, medium and small must be assessed based on some reference values, and if goals and targets are set, then these could form the basis for such reference values. The goals and targets must be based on observable quantities such as prices and production figures.

The total picture shows that the risk is of particular concern in relation to HES. There are large uncertainties associated with the effects of the chemical substances used and there is also a reputation-related aspect to this situation that one must keep in mind.

In addition, risk assessments are reported for the various areas isolated.

12.4   Risk treatment

How should the enterprise treat the risks? For the various areas, separate approaches are taken, for example, measures related to prices are made that are aimed at limiting or removing such risks. In the financial community, this is referred to as hedging.

An integrated analysis provides a good picture of what one can expect and where the uncertainties lie. Management is particularly concerned about the chemical problem and has decided to do something about this risk. Management applies a cautionary and precautionary way of thinking. There is significant uncertainty associated with the consequences, and with a view to what could possibly happen in the future, management chooses to pay the cost of changes and stop the use of the chemicals. The conclusion also has an ethical dimension – the enterprise feels that the staff should not be exposed to such a risk.

Reflection

Is it desirable to calculate a total risk index in the form of a number, which, in an appropriate way, will summarise the contributions from the various areas?

We are sceptical about this, because the risk picture associated with each area requires monitoring and follow-up, and the areas are so different. Whether such an index rises or falls will not be very informative, unless one looks into the aspects causing such a change.

13

Discussion

In this chapter, we discuss some factors that are important for ensuring that the risk analysis is carried out in a professional manner and provides adequate decision support. We have already pointed out many such factors in the earlier chapters. There is, however, a need to summarise the important points and expand the discussion of certain issues, for example, related to the strengths and weaknesses of the risk analyses. The following issues will be discussed:

- Risk analysis as a decision support tool: (i) the use of risk analysis in the decision-making process and (ii) the methods must be tailored to the analysis objectives.

- The importance of understanding that risk is more than calculated expected values and probabilities.

- The strong points and limitations of risk analysis.

- The importance of reflecting on approaches, methods and models.

- Limitations of the causal chain approach.

- Risk perspectives.

- Scientific basis.

- Critical systems and activities.

- On the difference between risk as seen from the perspectives of the analysts and management.

13.1 Risk analysis as a decision support tool

Risk analyses are carried out to provide decision-making support regarding choice of solutions and measures. Risk analysis does not give direct answers as to what is

Risk Analysis, Second Edition. Terje Aven.
© 2015 John Wiley & Sons, Ltd. Published 2015 by John Wiley & Sons, Ltd.

the correct solution and measure, but it only gives a risk description that will provide a basis for the choice of solutions or measures. The various examples given in Chapters 7–12 have demonstrated this fact. If a decision-making situation is not clearly formulated, the analysis should not be carried out. It makes no sense to assess risk after the decisions are made. Scheduling is therefore of great importance. The analysis must be carried out so that the results arrive in time. This, however, means that we have to carry out the analysis with limited knowledge of relevant systems and activities. Some seem to view this as a problem. They say the uncertainties are too large. However, such a conclusion is built on a misunderstanding of what a risk analysis is. The intent of a risk analysis is to systemise and describe the knowledge and the lack of knowledge one has concerning the phenomena and processes being studied. The fact that one is faced with large uncertainties is not a problem. The decision has to be made regardless of the level of uncertainty. Crude analyses that arrive at the right time are better than precise quantitative analyses that arrive too late.

Crude analyses (standard analyses) are, in many cases, also more suitable than model-based analyses, because they have the ability to capture in a qualitative way more relevant factors than the model-based analyses. The models often require strong simplifications, assumptions and suppositions, and this results in limited validity for the analysis. These models and their associated methods provide insights through comparisons of risk for the various alternatives and solutions, but one should not commence any detailed modelling if the decision problem does not require it. The analysis method must serve the objectives. Detailed analysis can easily mislead one into believing that the analysis has a higher precision level than it actually has and that there is no need to look beyond the calculations made. The risk analysis should provide decision-making support and, as a result, must have a level of detail that reflects what the decision is about. If the decision relates to maintenance, for example, the analysis must be capable of reflecting the scope/quality of the maintenance.

Incorporation of such factors and conditions can take place without detailed modelling in qualitative analyses. Alternatively, an attempt can be made to incorporate such conditions and factors explicitly into the analysis. This was done, for example, in the BORA method (Aven et al. 2006). The problem with such analyses is that they demand considerable effort and resources to develop suitable models and to express the risk. The cost involved is not necessarily in proportion to the usefulness of the analysis.

13.2   Risk is more than the calculated probabilities and expected values

To describe risk, it is not satisfactory to present one risk index, for example, an FAR value. This is illustrated by the Risk Level Norwegian Continental Shelf Project (Vinnem et al. 2006a), whose task was to describe risk for the total activities on the continental shelf. A number of methods to describe the risk were introduced: injury and accident statistics, risk indicators based on hazard situations, barrier indicators, risk analyses, interviews, surveys of co-workers and expert groups.

Generally, we would like the analysis to express risk for the total activity, but it should also reflect risk in relation to specific areas, groups, factors and so on.

The risk analyses conducted today often have a strong focus on probabilities and expected values. Reflections associated with the uncertainty dimension and manageability are lacking. Attention should also be paid to factors that influence the outcome and not only to the probability figures. A main message of this book is that risk is more than calculated probabilities and expected values. By focusing on the uncertainty dimension in the risk description, we could bring out conditions and factors that are not so easily covered by the risk calculations. We have shown a number of examples on this in Chapters 7–12. See also Chapter 2.

13.3   Risk analysis has both strengths and weaknesses

If risk analysis is to be used as intended, then its strengths and weaknesses must be understood.

A risk analysis is an analysis of risk. The analysis includes the identification and analysis of initiating events, cause analysis, consequence analysis and risk description. The aim of the analysis is to establish a risk picture for a given activity or a given system and, through this, to provide a basis for decision-making regarding the selection of solutions and measures. In particular, the analysis is aimed at identifying the important contributors to risk and describing the effect of possible measures on risk.

The risk analysis can be subdivided into various categories: simplified, standard and model-based. As long as the objective of the analysis is to analyse (understand, describe, etc.) risk, then it is a risk analysis.

The strength of the risk analysis is that it systemises available knowledge and uncertainties about phenomena, systems and activities that are being studied. What can go wrong, why and what are the consequences? This knowledge and this uncertainty are described and discussed, and thereby we obtain a basis on which we can evaluate what is important and compare different solutions and measures.

The risk analysis, however, also has some weaknesses, or should we say, limitations and challenges. Some of these are discussed in the following text.

13.3.1   Precision of a risk analysis: uncertainty and sensitivity analysis

If one has a large and relevant database, the probabilities derived from it could be precise in the sense that they may be able to provide accurate predictions of future events. For example, assume that one has observed 200 failures in a population of 10,000 units of type T over a 1-year period. The derived probability of failure for an arbitrarily chosen unit is 2%, and we will predict, for example, 20 failures per

1000 units. We can express the uncertainty, for example, using a 95% prediction interval: [11, 29]. The number of failures will lie within this interval with a 95% probability. To establish this interval, let X denote the number of failures among 1000 units. Then, X has a binomial distribution, which can be approximated by a normal distribution with a mean of 20 and standard deviation of 4.4, and this gives $P(11 \leq X \leq 29) = 0.95$ (see a textbook on statistics).

In a risk analysis context, we often focus on rare events, for example, the occurrence of a fatal accident, an accident that causes impairment of a main safety function and so on. We have only one unit or activity, and we are able to give a good prediction about the future: no fatal accidents will occur the next year. Fortunately, such a prediction will normally provide correct results. The risk analysis, however, should also express the likelihood associated with whether the event will occur. This raises the question about precision in the probability assignment.

Probability is used to express the analysts' uncertainty concerning whether the event will occur or not. If it is 10%, then the uncertainty is the same as drawing a particular ball from an urn containing 10 balls. It makes no sense discussing uncertainty in this number, but the assigned number depends, of course, on the assumptions and suppositions on which the analysis is built, and on who is carrying out the analysis. A critical question regarding the precision of the risk analysis results is thus in order.

The conclusion is that sensitivity analyses must be carried out in order to show how the results depend on various conditions and assumptions. Note that sensitivity analysis is not an analysis of uncertainty, as many seem to think. Sensitivity analysis highlights the importance of key quantities (parameters) and can provide a basis for assessing uncertainty. However, as such they do not provide any conclusions on uncertainties.

Many risk analyses today are characterised either by silence on the subject or by general statements such as:

> The analysis is based on the "best estimates" obtained by using the company's standards for models and data. It is acknowledged that there are uncertainties associated with all elements in the analysis, from the hazard identification to the models and probability calculations. It is concluded that the precision of the analysis is limited, and that one must take this into consideration when comparing the results with the risk acceptance criteria and tolerability limits.

The above statements are not very convincing, and they are not relevant to the risk perspective adopted in this book. It is obvious that there is no clarity regarding what the analysis express and what uncertainty means in a risk analysis context.

In any event, does this acknowledgement – that a considerable amount of uncertainty exists – affect the analysis and the conclusions? Only very rarely! Our impression is that one writes such statements just to meet a requirement, and then they are put aside. This says a lot about the quality of the analysis.

In cases where we have observed data, we can compare the risk figures with these. Do the risk figures give reasonable predictions of the number of events? If the analysis yields a probability figure that, for example, indicates 10 leakages of a certain category over 20 years, but observed data for similar systems is an order of magnitude lower, then this must be discussed. Is the result reasonable or is there a need to have a closer look at the uncertainty assessments? Rarely do we see that such reflections are carried out in the risk analyses of today.

The precision level of the analysis is important for how the risk analysis can, and should, be used. There is, for example, no use in applying the analysis for *precise* comparisons of the results with given limits to decide whether the risk is acceptable. If we wish to compare with a criterion of $1 \cdot 10^{-4}$, we cannot in practice distinguish between the results from risk analyses that yield values of, for example, $2 \cdot 10^{-4}$, and $0.5 \cdot 10^{-4}$. The results are in the same order of magnitude as the criterion, and there is no need to say more.

13.3.2   Terminology

Risk is often presented in a way that is difficult to understand. The definitions used are often imprecise and unclear. Two examples of typical definitions of individual risk (group individual risk) are given as follows:

> Individual risks are calculated as frequency of death for a person or critical group of personnel most at risk from a given activity as a result of their location, habits or time period which make them vulnerable.

> The annual frequency of an accident with one or more fatalities averaged over a homogenous group of people.

The intended meaning is probably this: the probability that a randomly chosen person in the group will be killed during his/her stay at the facility over the course of the time period considered.

However, how is one to obtain a meaningful analysis, when one cannot even define with precision what is being calculated?

Example of an improper application of the risk matrix

The risk matrix is a tool for describing risk, it is not a risk analysis method. In this section, we provide an example of an improper use of the risk matrix as an analysis tool. Assume that we are carrying out a risk analysis of functions/systems that are critical for the community. The analysis group presents a risk matrix as shown in Figure 13.1. The consequences and probabilities (frequencies) are categorised on a scale from 1 to 5. A risk index is defined, based on the product of the probability category and the consequence category. The lowest risk is represented by number 1 and the highest risk by number 25.

	Category	Consequence – number of fatalities				
		≤ 5 1	6–50 2	51–300 3	301–1000 4	>1000 5
Probability > once per year	5	5	10	15	20	25
1–3 times per 10 years	4	4	Difference: 4		16	20
1–3 times every 100 years	3	3	6	9	12	15
1–3 times every 500 years	2	4	4	Difference: 5		10
< once every 500 years	1	1	2	3	4	5

Figure 13.1   Improper use of the risk matrix, with scores based on categories 1–5.

	Per year	Consequence – number of fatalities				
		≤ 5 2.5	6–50 28	51–300 175	301–1000 650	>1000 1.200
Probability > once per year	2	5	56	350	1300	2400
1–3 times per 10 years	0.2	0.5	Difference: 117		130	240
1–3 times every 100 years	0.02	0.05	0.56	3.5	13	24
1–3 times every 500 years	0.004	0.01	0.112	Difference: 3.6		4.8
< once every 500 years	0.001	0.0025	0.028	0.17	0.65	1.2

Figure 13.2   Risk matrix, with scores based on the expected number of fatalities.

The focus of the analysis is on two different risk-reducing measures, and the two arrows show the effect of these measures. The analysis will be used to select one of these measures for implementation. According to the analysis, Measure 1 reduces the probability from category 4 to category 3 (consequence category 4). Measure 2 reduces the probability from category 2 to category 1 (consequence category 5). We see that Measure 1 gives a risk reduction of 4 "risk units," whereas Measure 2 gives a risk reduction of 5 "risk units." The difference between the two measures appears small, but let us assume that the analysis group, on the basis of these results, recommends implementing Measure 2 – it gives the largest risk reduction. We assume that other factors such as cost, environmental effects and so on, are not relevant.

Figure 13.2 shows the same example, but the score is now the mid-point in the probability and consequence categories instead of categories 1–5. We see that the mid-point in the frequency categories follows approximately a logarithmic scale, that is, the increase is about 10-fold for each category. Likewise, we see that the mid-point in the consequence categories increases by about fivefold for each category. This means that they are not logarithmic, but "close" to logarithmic.

Let us assume that the analysis group chooses to express risk as the product of consequence and frequency (probability), that is, the expected number of fatalities over one year (PLL). We then obtain the risk figures shown in the matrix of Figure 13.2. Let us now compare the two measures based on these risk figures. Measure 1 reduces the number of expected fatalities per year from 130 to 13, in other words, a reduction in PLL of 117. Measure 2 reduces PLL from 4.8 to 1.2, that is, a reduction of PLL of 3.6. Here, we can see that the difference in risk reduction for the two measures is large. In this case, it would be obvious for the analysis group to recommend implementation of Measure 1 (if risk alone is considered) since the difference in risk reduction for the two measures is significant.

From the example, we see that the two analysis methods lead to different conclusions: the first method identifies Measure 2 as the best one, but only just, while the other method identifies Measure 1 as the best by far, in terms of risk.

Why do the results differ so much? The reason is that we have (almost) logarithmic scales in the second example, which was not taken into consideration in the first example where we used categories 1–5. The analysis based on categories 1–5 suggests that the category at the top right of the matrix has 25 times the risk as that at the bottom left. This sounds very high. But if we use logarithmic categories, then this difference becomes much larger. This is the reason why the two measures emerge as almost equal in the first example and widely different in the second. The categorisation 1–5 works just fine as long as we use the risk matrix to present the analysis results. However, the moment we use it to analyse the benefits of the measure, it is easy to commit method-related errors. From the example, we note the following:

- We must be careful when introducing quantities that are difficult to explain and justify, such as the categorisation 1–5.

- The risk matrix is a tool for presentation, not for analysis. The results of the analysis, and hence the recommendations for the decision-maker, change depending on the design of the matrix.

13.3.3   Risk acceptance criteria (tolerability limits)

To manage risk, and in particular safety, it is common to use a hierarchy of goals, criteria and requirements, such as the following:

A. Overall ideal goals, for example "our goal is to have no accidents."

B. Risk acceptance criteria (defined as upper limits of acceptable risk) or tolerability limits, controlling the accident risk, for example "the individual probability of being killed in an accident shall not exceed 0.1%."

C. Requirements related to the performance of safety systems and barriers, such as reliability requirement for a safety system.

D. Requirements related to the specific design and operation of a component or subsystem, for example, the gas detection system.

According to the standard procedures for using such goals, criteria and requirements, they are to be specified before alternatives are generated and subsequently analysed. The point is to look for what to obtain before looking for possible ways of implementation. For example, the Norwegian offshore petroleum regulations state that risk acceptance criteria (expressed as upper limits of acceptable risk) should be developed and that this should be done before the risk analyses are carried out (PSA 2001, Aven and Vinnem 2007). Note that in the following discussion, when using the term "risk acceptance criteria," we always refer to such upper limits.

Are such criteria appropriate for managing risk? Consider the following criterion: "The probability of having an oil spill during 1 year of operation causing an environmental damage having a restitution period of more than z years should not exceed $1 \cdot 10^{-x}$."

At the political level, it is obvious that it would not be possible to establish consensus about such a limit. Different parties would have different preferences. But for the government would it be possible to establish such a number? Say that it would make an attempt to do this. And suppose that it considers two options, a weak limit, say $1 \cdot 10^{-3}$, and a strong limit, say $1 \cdot 10^{-4}$. What limit should it choose? The answer would be the weak limit, as the strong limit could mean lack of flexibility in choosing the overall best solution. If the benefits are sufficiently large, the level $1 \cdot 10^{-3}$ could be acceptable. Following this line of argument, the use of such limits leads to the formulation of weak limits, which are met in most situations. Risk analysis is then used to verify that the risk is acceptable in relation to these weak limits. It is, to a large extent, a waste of money; the conclusion is obvious.

At the operational level, the same type of arguments will apply. The oil company is to determine an acceptance criterion, and it faces the same type of dilemma as above. Why should it specify strong limits? It would restrict the company from obtaining the overall best solution. The result is that weak limits are specified and risk analyses play the role of verification, a role that does not add much value.

If a high level of safety is to be obtained, mechanisms other than risk acceptance criteria need to be implemented, such as ALARP processes. If such criteria are established, they give a focus on obtaining a minimum safety standard – with no drive for improvement and risk reduction.

We conclude that care has to be shown when introducing risk acceptance criteria. Risk should not be considered in isolation. We do not accept the risk, but options that entail some level of risk among their consequences (Fischhoff et al. 1981, p.3). Principally speaking, a requirement (criterion) related to risk and safety cannot be isolated from what the solution and measure mean in relation to other attributes, in particular costs. It is impossible to know what should be the proper requirement without knowing what it implies and what it means when it comes to cost, effect on safety and so on. In other words, we first need the alternatives. Then, we can analyse and evaluate them, and, finally, we should make a decision.

This is our theoretical position. It applies to all levels of limits (within categories B and C mentioned earlier) from the high-level performance of an industry, a plant and so on, to the detailed equipment level. In practice, however, there is a need for a more pragmatic thinking about the use of such criteria and requirements, in particular, for more detailed requirements, as explained in the following text.

When designing a complex system such as an offshore installation, we need to introduce some simplifications. We simplify the description of the installation by saying that it consists of several systems (the word "system" is used here in a broad sense, covering aspects of structure, layout, emergency preparedness, etc.). For all these systems, there are possible detailed arrangements and measures. However, in an early design phase, it is not feasible to specify all these arrangements and measures in detail, and instead we use some sort of performance characterisation. Typically, these will be industry standards, established practice and descriptions of the performance of the system, given by reliability, effectiveness (capacity) and robustness. In other words, instead of specifying in an accurate way what system we need, we specify the performance of the system. Thus, we basically have three levels of specification:

1. the installation comprising its arrangements and measures (this is the way the installation will be in operation);

2. the installation described by systems defined through a form of performance characterisations and

3. systems described by specific arrangements and measures.

Level 1 is the ultimate level – the installation as it would be in the future. In an early planning phase, we may use Level 2 and specify systems and their performance. In detailed design, we move to Level 3 and specify the detailed and specific arrangements and measures for the relevant system. Specifying performance requirements related to Level 3 is not a problem, since they simply express properties of the arrangements and measures. The interesting question is whether we can justify the use of performance requirements at Level 2. Our conclusion is that such requirements are necessary for the practical execution of the project. We need some starting point for the specification of the performance for the system level. Consider the following example:

> Safety system reliability requirement: "Safety system S shall have a maximum failure on demand probability equal to 1%."

Instead of a sharp level, ranges may also be used, such as the categorisation used for Safety Integrity Level (SIL) requirements, in accordance with IEC 61511 (2003), for example a failure probability in the range of 10–1%. The engineering process will produce a specific system layout that should meet this requirement. The starting point for choosing a certain requirement could be historical data, standards or the desire to achieve a certain risk level or improvement.

For the 1% requirement to be meaningful, it must not be seen as a sharp line; we should always look for alternatives and then evaluate their performance. Whether the analysis team calculates a reliability of 0.2, 0.5 or 2% is not so important – depending on the situation, we may accept all these levels. The interesting question is how the alternatives perform relatively, concerning reliability, cost and other factors. The number 1% must be seen as a starting point for further optimisation.

This section can be summarised as follows: one should avoid using pre-defined risk acceptance criteria for managing risk at a high system level, such as an industry or a plant. On a more detailed system level, criteria and requirements need to be introduced to simplify the project development process. However, the criteria and requirements defined should not be seen as strict limits. There should always be a drive for generating overall better alternatives.

13.4   Reflection on approaches, methods and results

Only very rarely we do see reflections about the approaches, methods and models used in risk analyses. How good and suitable are the models used? The problem that many analysts surely struggle with in this regard is that they do not know how to deal with this issue. They are supposed to carry out an analysis and use those methods and models that the company or the enterprise has. Problems related to the selection of methods and models undermine, in a sense, the authority and the message of the analysis. So, if the client/employer is not aware of the problem, then it will not be addressed.

The models are used as tools to obtain insights into risk, to express risk and form part of the conditions and the background knowledge on which the analysis is built. It is no less important to reflect on how suitable the model is for its objective. In this regard, however, it is not only the approximation of the real world that is the point, but also the model's ability to reflect the essential aspects of the real world and to simplify complicated features and conditions.

Data quality is more often discussed, but also here, the discussion is, in many instances, too superficial.

As discussed above, the results from the analysis are often presented without reflection on what contributes to the risk, how sensitive the results are to changes in the input data and so on. This is unfortunate as it gives the impression that the results are more accurate than they actually are.

13.5   Limitations of the causal chain approach

The traditional risk analysis approach can be viewed as a special case of system engineering (Haimes 2004). This approach, which to a large extent is based on causal chains and event modelling, has been subject to strong criticism. Many researchers argue that some of the key methods used in risk analysis are not able to capture "systemic accidents." Hollnagel (2004), for example, argues that to model systemic accidents it is necessary to go beyond the causal chains – we must describe system performance as a whole, where the steps and stages on the way to an accident are seen as parts of a whole rather than as distinct events. It is interesting not only to model the events that lead to the occurrence of an accident, which is done in, for example, event trees and fault trees, but also to capture the array of factors at different system levels that contribute to the occurrence of these events. Leveson (2007) makes her points very clear:

> Traditional methods and tools for risk analysis and management have not been terribly successful in the new types of high-tech systems with distributed human and automated decision-making we are attempting to build today. The traditional approaches, mostly based on viewing causality in terms of chains of events with relatively simple cause-effect links, are based on assumptions that do not fit these new types of systems: These approaches to safety engineering were created in the world of primarily mechanical systems and then adapted for electro-mechanical systems, none of which begin to approach the level of complexity, non-linear dynamic interactions, and technological innovation in today's socio-technical systems. At the same time, today's complex engineered systems have become increasingly essential to our lives. In addition to traditional infrastructures (such as water, electrical, and ground transportation systems), there are increasingly complex communication systems, information systems, air transportation systems, new product/process development systems, production systems, distribution systems and others.
>
> The limitations of the traditional models and approaches to managing and assessing risk in these systems make it difficult to include all factors contributing to risk, including human performance and organizational, management and social factors; to incorporate human error and complex decision-making; and to capture the non-linear dynamics of interactions among components, including the adaptation of social and technical structures over time.

Leveson argues for a paradigm-changing approach to safety engineering and risk management. She refers to a new alternative accident model, called STAMP (System-Theoretic Accident Modelling and Processes).

A critical review of the principles and methods being used is , of course, important, and the research by Rasmussen (1997), Hollnagel and Leveson in this field adds valuable input to the further development of risk analysis as a discipline. Obviously, we need a set of different approaches and methods for analysing risk.

No approach is able to meet the expectations with respect to all aspects. The causal chains and event modelling approach has been shown to work for a number of industries and settings, and the overall judgement of the approach is not as negative as Leveson expresses. Furthermore, the causal chains and event modelling approach is continuously improved, incorporating human, operational and organisational factors; see for example, I-Risk (Papazoglou et al. 2003), ARAMIS (Duijm and Goossens, 2006), the BORA project (Aven et al. 2006), the SAM approach (Paté-Cornell and Murphy 1996) and more recently Mohaghegh et al. (2009). It is not difficult to point at the limitations of these approaches, but it is important to acknowledge that the suitability of a model always has to be judged with reference to not only its ability to represent the real world but also its ability to simplify the world. All models are wrong, but they can still be useful to use a well-known phrase.

The approach taken in this book is partly based on the causal chains and event modelling. However, we acknowledge the limitations of this approach, as well as other aspects of the analyses, and add alternative qualitative tools to see beyond these limitations. Insights provided by this alternative research paradigm can be used to strengthen the risk picture obtained by the more traditional approach. The framework adopted in this book allows for such an extended knowledge basis. In fact, it encourages the analysts to search for such a basis.

13.6   Risk perspectives

There is no agreed definition of risk. Risk is understood as an expected value, a probability distribution, as uncertainty and as an event. Some common definitions are (Aven and Renn 2009a):

1. Risk equals the expected loss (Willis 2007).

2. Risk equals the expected disutility (Campbell 2005)

3. Risk is the probability of an adverse outcome (Graham and Weiner 1995).

4. Risk is a measure of the probability and severity of adverse effects (Lowrance 1976).

5. Risk is the effect of uncertainty on objectives (ISO 2009a,b).

6. Risk is defined as a set of scenarios s_i, each of which has a probability p_i and a consequence c_i (Kaplan and Garrick 1981, Kaplan 1991).

7. Risk is equal to the two-dimensional combination of events/consequences and associated uncertainties (Aven 2007a, and this book).

8. Risk refers to uncertainty of outcome, actions and events (Cabinet Office 2002).

9. Risk is a situation or event where something of human value (including humans themselves) is at stake and where the outcome is uncertain (Rosa 1998, 2003).

10. Risk is an uncertain consequence of an event or an activity with respect to something that human beings value (Renn 2005).

11. Risk is uncertainty about and severity of the consequences of an activity, with respect to something that human beings value (Aven and Renn 2009a, b).

12. Risk refers to situations with known probabilities for the randomness the decision-maker is faced with (Knight 1921, Douglas 1983).

It is common to refer to risk as probability multiplied by consequences (losses), that is, what is called the *expected value* in probability calculus. If C is the quantity of interest, for example the number of future attacks, number of fatalities, cost and so on, the expected value would be a good representation of risk if this value is approximately equal to C, that is, $EC \approx C$. But since C is unknown at the time of assessment, how can we be sure that this approximation would be accurate? Can the law of large numbers (Aven 2012d), which says that the empirical mean of independent identically distributed random variables converges to the expected value when the number of variables increases to infinity, be applied? Or could we apply the portfolio theory (Levy and Sarnat 1990), which says that the value of a portfolio of projects is approximately equal to the expected value, plus the systematic risk (uncertainties) caused by events affecting the whole market, be applied?

Yes, it is likely that if C is the sum of the number of projects, or some average number, our expected value could be a good prediction of C. Take, for example, the number of fatalities in traffic in a specific country. From the previous years we have data that can be used to accurately predict the number of fatalities next year (C). In Norway, about 150 people were killed last year, and using this number as EC and predictor for the coming year, we would be quite sure that this number is relatively close to the actual C.

However, in many cases, the uncertainties are much larger. Looking at the number of fatalities in Norway caused by terrorist attacks the next year, the historical data would give a poor basis. We may assign an EC but obviously EC could be far away from C. The accuracy increases when we extend the population of interest. If we look at one unit (e.g. country) in isolation, the C number is in general more uncertain than if we consider many units (e.g. countries). Yet, there will always be uncertainties, and in a world where the speed of change is increasing, relevant historical data are scarce and will not be sufficient to obtain accurate predictions.

Even so, some researchers define risk by the expected values. Consider the terrorism case discussed in Willis (2007). Willis (2007) defines risk as follows:

> Terrorism risk: The expected consequences of an existent threat, which for a given target, attack mode, target vulnerability and damage type, can be expressed as

Risk = P(attack occurs) $\cdot$ P(attacks results in damage | attacks occurs)
$\cdot E$[damage | attacks occurs and results in damage]

Willis (2007) refers to Haimes (2004), who highlights that expected value decision-making is misleading for rare and extreme events. The expected value (the mean or the central tendency) does not adequately capture events with low probabilities and high consequences (Haimes 2004, p. 41). Nonetheless, Willis (2007) represents risk by the expected value as the basis for his analysis. The motivation seems to be that the expected value provides a suitable practical approach for comparing and aggregating terrorism risk, as it is based on just one number.

For terrorism risk, where the possible consequences could be extreme and the uncertainties in underlying phenomena and processes are so large, it is obvious that the expected value may hide important aspects of concern for risk management. The expected value can be small, say 0.01 fatalities, but extreme events with millions of fatalities may occur, and this needs special attention.

One way of representing this aspect of risk is to specify the probability of an event resulting in large damages, P(large damages), for example, the probability of occurrence of an event that leads to a large number of fatalities. Willis notes that estimates of such probabilities of the worst-case outcomes, captured in the tail of the distribution of consequences, will be very dependent on assumptions when considering events such as terrorism where there are large uncertainties about events and limited historical information.

However, estimates of the risk defined by the expected value will be strongly dependent on the assumptions made. Willis acknowledges this and he remarks in several instances in his paper that there are large uncertainties in the risk estimates. Willis' thinking seems to be based on the idea that there exists a true probability and a true risk. He speaks about errors in risk estimates, which means that there must be a reference point (a true value) to judge deviation. For the probability of attack, Willis emphasises that this probability is uncertain and that one should keep in mind that it can also be represented by a probability distribution and not a point estimate.

Certainly, if the risk perspective adopted is based on the idea of a true risk, the uncertainties in the estimates would be extremely large in a terrorism risk case. And these uncertainties need to be taken into account in the risk management. Willis claims that the conclusions drawn in his study are robust to these uncertainties, but this is hard to see, and it is obvious that in general the uncertainties would be so large that the risk management would be affected.

The idea of a true probability fits into a classical relative frequency paradigm; a probability is interpreted as the relative fraction of times the events occur if the situation analysed were hypothetically "repeated" an infinite number of times. The underlying probability is unknown and is estimated in the risk analysis. But is such an interpretation meaningful for the terrorism risk case? Can P(attack occurs) be understood by reference to such a thought-constructed repeated experiment? No, it cannot. It has no meaning.

The alternative, and the adopted perspective in this book (the so-called Bayesian perspective or approach), is to consider probability as a measure of uncertainty about events and outcomes (consequences), seen through the eyes of the assessor and based on some background information and knowledge. However, as stressed in Chapter 2, probability is not a perfect tool for this purpose. The assigned probabilities are conditional on a specific background knowledge, and they could produce poor predictions.

This leads to the conclusion that the main component of risk is uncertainty and not probability – uncertainty about attacks occurring and about the resulting damages.

Based on this acknowledgement, we conclude that there is a need for a broad approach to risk, as described in this book. To evaluate the seriousness of risk and conclude on risk treatment, we need to see beyond the expected values and the probabilities. This is also in line with other approaches, including the UK Cabinet office approach (Cabinet Office 2002) and the risk governance framework (Renn 2005).

We refer to Aven et al. (2011) for a discussion of the differences between definition (11) and Rosa (1998)'s definition (9) and Renn's (2005) definition (10). A main point is that the restriction of the risk concept to events and consequences means that several fundamental concepts need to be reinterpreted.

Our definition does not include utilities as in definition (2). The preferences of the decision-maker is not a part of the risk concept. There will be a strong degree of arbitrariness in the choice of the utility function, and some decision-makers would also be reluctant to specify the utility function as it reduces their flexibility to weigh different concerns in specific cases.

An alternative approach for analysing intelligent attacks is to use game theory; see Guikema (2009) and the references therein. Using this approach, possible interactions are taken into account, but strong assumptions need to be made related to the attackers' behaviour and decision-making. We refer the reader to Guikema and Aven (2010).

13.7   Scientific basis

We consider a risk problem where the uncertainties are large. To be specific, think about the examples in Chapters 7–12, or the terrorism example. If the goal of the analysis is to obtain accurate estimates of some true risk, we can quickly conclude that risk analysis fails as a scientific method. Referring to the previous section, we can conclude that the classical approach to risk analysis does not work in situations involving large uncertainties. The uncertainties of the risk estimates are too large.

Alternatively, we may consider risk analysis as a tool for assessing uncertainties about risk and risk estimates. Since the assessment's aim is then to express uncertainties about the true risk, focus is not on the accuracy in the risk estimates but rather the "accuracy" of the transformation of uncertainties to probabilities. Risk analysis is then not about bounding and reducing uncertainties but to describe uncertainties. Two prevailing approaches for describing the uncertainties are given as follows:

1. Traditional statistical methods such as confidence interval.

2. The probability of frequency approach, that is, assessing epistemic uncertainties about the risk by means of subjective probabilities. In this approach, there are two levels of probability introduced: (i) the relative frequency interpreted probabilities reflecting variation within populations and (ii) the knowledge-based (subjective) probabilities reflecting the analyst's uncertainty about what the correct relative frequency probabilities are (see e.g. Kaplan and Garrick (1981) and Aven (2012d)). In Garrick et al. (2004), the probability of frequency approach is suggested for risk analysis of terrorist attacks. Garrick et al. (2004) refers to a probability distribution in which there is a probability of 20% that the attackers would succeed in 10% of their attacks.

However, confidence intervals would not work in this setting as we do not have sufficient amount of relevant data. Even if some data are available, the traditional statistical approach is problematic. To apply the approach, probability models like the normal distribution and the log normal distribution need to be specified, but in practice it is difficult to determine the appropriate distribution. Our historical data may include no extreme observations, but this does not preclude such observations from occurring in the future. Statistical analysis, including Bayesian statistics, is based on the idea of similar situations, and if "similar" is limited to the historical data, the population considered could be far too small or narrow. However, by extending the population, the statistical framework breaks down. There is no justification for such an extended probability model. The statistician needs a probability model to be able to perform a statistical analysis, and then he will base his analysis on the data available. Taleb (2007) refers to the worlds of mediocristan and extremistan to explain the difference between the standard probability model context and the more extended population required to reflect surprises occurring in the future, respectively. Without explicitly formulating the thesis, Taleb (2007) is saying that we have to see beyond the historically based probability models. See also Aven (2014).

The ambition of the probability of frequency approach is to express the epistemic uncertainties of the probability p of an attack and take into account all relevant factors causing uncertainties. The analysis may produce a 90% credibility interval for p, $[a, b]$, saying that the analyst is 90% confident that p lies in the interval $[a, b]$. In practice, it is difficult to perform a complete uncertainty analysis following this approach. In theory, an uncertainty distribution on the total model and parameter space should be established, which is impossible to do. So, in applications only a few marginal distributions on some selected parameters are normally specified, and, therefore, the uncertainty distributions on the output probabilities are just reflecting some aspects of the uncertainty. This makes it difficult to interpret the uncertainties produced.

The validity of the risk analysis when adopting the probability of frequency approach can also be questioned, from a different angle. As questioned in the previous section, is the relative frequency interpreted probability of an attack p really the quantity of interest? Our goal is to express the risk of an activity or system, but in this approach we are concerned about the average performance of a thought-constructed population of similar situations. Are these quantities meaningful representations of the activity or system being studied? Clearly, for example, when looking at the total activity of a society or a nation, it is hard to understand the meaning of such a constructed infinite population. If we are to assess uncertainties concerning average performance of quantities of such populations, it is essential that we understand what they mean.

According to the approach adopted in this book, probability is a measure of uncertainty seen through the eyes of the assessor and based on the background knowledge. The aim of risk analysis in this context is to assess and express uncertainties about unknown quantities using probabilities.

Properly conducted, such an approach meets the validity requirement: the risk analysis predicts these quantities and assesses uncertainties, that is, it describes the concepts that one is attempting to describe. Of course, the observables addressed should be informative in the sense that the results of the analysis support the decision-making. If this is not the case, there is obviously a validity problem. Furthermore, as for the probability of frequency approach, important uncertainty factors may easily be hidden in the background knowledge and the uncertainty assessments may not be complete, also causing a validity problem.

For further reading on this topic, see Aven and Heide (2009), Aven (2011a).

We see that the scientific basis of risk assessments can be questioned, depending on the risk perspective adopted. We discuss the implications for risk management in the next section.

13.8   The implications of the limitations of risk assessment

Apostolakis and Lemon (2005) adopt a pragmatic approach to risk analysis and risk management, acknowledging the difficulties of determining probabilities for an attack. Ideally, they would like to implement a risk-informed procedure, based on expected values. However, since such an approach would require the use of probabilities that have not been "derived rigorously," they see themselves forced to resort to a more pragmatic approach.

This is one possible approach when facing problems of large uncertainties. The risk analyses simply do not provide a sufficient solid basis for the decision-making process. Others, however, conclude differently as already mentioned. Garrick et al. (2004) recommend the use of the probability of frequency approach, despite the problems of implementing this approach as discussed in the previous section (see also

Aven (2007a)). In our view, a full probabilistic analysis as in the probability of frequency approach cannot be justified. In a risk evaluation, we need to see beyond the computed risk picture in the form of the summarising probabilities and expected values, as discussed in previous sections. Traditional quantitative risk analyses fail in this respect. We acknowledge the need for analysing risk, but question the value added by performing traditional quantitative risk analyses in cases of large uncertainties. The arbitrariness in the numbers produced could be significant, due to the uncertainties in the estimates or as a result of the uncertainty assessments being strongly dependent on the analysts.

We should acknowledge that risk cannot be accurately expressed using probabilities and expected values. A quantitative risk analysis is in many cases better replaced by a more qualitative approach, as adopted in this book. We may refer to it as a semi-quantitative approach.

Quantifying risk by using risk indices such as the expected number of fatalities gives an impression that risk can be expressed in a very precise way. However, in most cases, the arbitrariness is large, and our semi-quantitative approach acknowledges this by providing a more nuanced risk picture, which includes factors that can cause "surprises" relative to the probabilities and the expected values. We are not negative to detailed risk quantification as such, but quantification often requires strong simplifications and assumptions and, as a result, important factors could be ignored or given too little (or much) weight. In a qualitative or semi-quantitative analysis, a more comprehensive risk picture can be established taking into account the underlying factors influencing risk. In contrast to the prevailing use of quantitative risk analyses, the precision level of the risk description is in line with the accuracy of the risk analysis tools. In addition, risk quantification is very resource demanding. We need to ask whether the resources are used in the best way. We conclude that in many cases more is gained by opening up for a broader, more qualitative approach, which allows for considerations beyond the probabilities and expected values.

This approach highlights the uncertainty component of risk, in line with our perspective of risk. For problems with large uncertainties, risk analyses could support decision-making, but other principles, measures and instruments are required. We refer to Section 1.2.1 and, in particular, to the cautionary principle, which is a basic principle in risk and safety management, expressing that in the face of uncertainty, caution should be a ruling principle, for example, by not starting an activity, or by implementing measures to reduce risks and uncertainties.

Reflection

Can the risk analyses be carried out if we do not have access to a large amount of historical data?

Yes, risk analyses can always be carried out. Risk can always be expressed, regardless of access to input data. Through the risk analysis, the knowledge and lack of knowledge one has concerning various quantities are expressed. In such a case, it will be difficult, however, to establish good predictions, and the uncertainties could be large.

13.9   Critical systems and activities

To support decision-making concerning safety and security issues, identification of critical systems (activities) is considered an important task. The motivation for identifying the critical systems is the need for prioritising activities and resources on safety and security investments and risk-reduction processes. If a list of critical systems have been identified, the management tasks can focus on the systems on this list.

Different approaches have been suggested for this purpose. Basically, we may distinguish between the following two categories: a system or activity is critical (i) if the vulnerability is high or (ii) if the risk is high.

The first type of interpretation is the most common. A typical definition is the following: A system is considered critical if its failure or malfunction may result in severe consequences, for example, related to loss of lives, environmental damage or economic loss (Falla 1997). Recently, there has been a special focus on critical infrastructure; see Gheorghe et al. (2006) and RESS (2007) and the references therein. A critical infrastructure can be defined as "organisations and facilities of key importance to public interest whose failure or impairment could result in detrimental supply shortages, substantial disturbance to public order or similar dramatic impact" (Gheorghe et al. 2006). The US National Infrastructure Protection Plan (NIPP) states that: "critical infrastructure are systems and assets, whether physical or virtual, so vital to the Nation that the incapacity or destruction of such systems and assets would have a debilitating impact on national economic security, and/or public health or safety, or any combination of those matters." However, there are other definitions and these are just examples to illustrate what is typically meant by critical infrastructure. The following is a more general definition of a critical system in a societal context (Gheorghe et al. 2006, p. 26): A critical system is a system that, when failing, would seriously disrupt society.

The second category of criticality measures includes the probability of the initiating event. As an example, we refer to Jenelius et al. (2006), who define criticality as the product of probability and importance (conditional criticality), where importance reflects the increase in travel cost when a link in the network is closed. This category also incorporates traditional risk and reliability importance measures; see, for example, Modarres (1993) and Aven and Jensen (1999). Two of the most common measures are Birnbaums's measure and the improvement potential (also referred to as the *risk reduction worth*) (Aven (2012d), van der Borst and Schoonakker 2001). The former measure is defined by the sensitivity (partial derivative) of the reliability (risk) with respect to parameters, for example, the reliability of a safety barrier. The latter measure expresses the risk contribution from a specific system, determined by calculating the difference in the risk indices when assuming that the system has no failures or malfunctions.

Including the probability and uncertainty dimension is in the core of the risk analysis tradition, and risk analysts may consider this statement obvious. However, there are different traditions and ways of thinking (paradigms) concerning this issue as discussed above. In security applications, it is often assumed that the vulnerabilities will be exposed with probability 1.0, so there is no need for including the probability dimension in the analysis.

We consider two examples: the identification of safety critical systems in a process plant and the identification of critical infrastructures.

Example 1: identifying safety critical systems

In a process plant there are a number of safety systems, and to reveal the state of these systems, inspection and testing are required. As an example, we may think of the system as a safety valve and our concern is leakages through the valve. The inspection and testing is resource demanding and means production shutdown. The management proposes to introduce a classification scheme that can identify the most critical systems so that the risk management activities can focus on these systems. The identified safety critical systems are to provide a basis for determining suitable inspection and testing policies. If a system is defined as safety critical, more frequent inspection and testing are required than if the system is not defined as critical. But what do we mean by critical?

As mentioned above, a common practice is to say that the system is critical if its failure or malfunction may result in severe consequences, such as loss of lives, environmental damage or economic loss. Say that a system (System 1) has three failure modes, with the following conditional expected consequences:

Failure mode	Expected consequences (given failure)
f_1	1-day shutdown
f_2	2-day shutdown
f_3	100-day shutdown

Another system (System 2) has the following expected consequences:

Failure mode	Expected consequences (given failure)
f_4	0.1-day shutdown
f_5	10-day shutdown
f_6	10-day shutdown

The difference could reflect that the systems simply have different characteristics – they are two different types of equipment, or it could reflect that the systems have different positions in the overall process plant network of systems and equipment. Due to redundancy, the consequences of failures do not immediately cause shutdown.

Based on the above conditional expected consequences, which system is most critical? It depends, of course, on the rationale being adopted. Looking at the worst expected consequence, we see that System 1 is the most critical. But System 2 leads to a shutdown duration of 10 days for two failure modes, and these failure modes may be much more likely to occur than f_3. Should we not take that into account?

Furthermore, the consequence categories are expected values, which means that different outcomes could be observed. If the failure mode is simply leakage, we may consider the scenario defined by leakage resulting in a specific severe consequence. This would lead to a higher shutdown duration, but of course a lower probability of occurrence. We see that the expected consequences depend very much on the definition of the failure mode.

The calculated expected consequences could produce poor predictions of the actual consequences (outcomes) if the failure mode considered could result in a set of different outcomes or if the underlying uncertainties in the consequences of system failures are large. To explain this, assume that the possible consequences of a system failure mode are 20, 100 or 400, with associated probabilities 0.6, 0.3 and 0.1. Then, the expected value equals 82. Clearly, 82 could be a poor prediction of the actual outcome, which is either 20, 100 or 400.

The expected consequences are based on an isolated system failure analysis. Other systems are assumed to operate normal, that is, they may fail, but in expectation the contributions from multiple failures will be small. Hence, if the system considered is in parallel with another system, the expected consequences will be small compared to a case where the system considered is in series with this other system. Obviously, this kind of analysis may hide that failure events may occur with extreme consequences. As long as the expected consequences are focused, the full spectre of possible consequences are not revealed.

In addition, the probabilities are not objective numbers and the background information for the analysts' assignments (assumptions and knowledge) could be poor and could result in inaccurate predictions of the actual outcomes.

Hence, by focusing on the expected consequences given a failure mode, a strong element of arbitrariness is introduced in the classification scheme. This arbitrariness is due to the variation in possible outcomes integrated into the expected value, as well as the difficulty of assigning probabilities producing accurate predictions.

We see that a criticality classification based on this way of thinking has strong limitations. Care has to be shown when using vulnerability as the basis for the criticality ranking.

This leads to a risk-informed approach, while taking into account the probabilities of the initiating events – in this case the probability of system failure. Let A denote such an event and p the probability that A occurs. Furthermore, let C denote the consequences associated with an occurrence of A. For the sake of simplicity, assume that the consequences are linked to production downtimes only. Then, we can define a suitable risk index expressing criticality. Two obvious candidates are:

1. Expected loss (downtime) $E[C]$, given by $p \cdot E[C|A]$, that is, the product of the probability of A and the expected loss given that A occurs.

2. Expected disutility $Eu(C)$, where u is a utility function reflecting the preferences of the decision-maker.

The motivation for using $E[C]$ is that the expected loss provides a suitable practical approach for comparing and aggregating risk, as it is based on just one number. By reference to the law of large numbers, the expected value provides an accurate prediction of the actual loss when considering a large number of independent projects (refer Section 13.6). However, the expected value is not necessarily in line with the preferences of the decision-maker, who may be risk averse in the sense that he dislikes uncertainties more than what the expected value is reflecting. Using the expected disutility, this kind of risk aversion can be taken into account.

Defining risk and criticality with reference to the expected loss means that there is no distinction made between situations involving potential large consequences and associated small probabilities, and frequently occurring events with rather small consequences, as long as the product of the possible outcomes and the probabilities are equal. For risk management, these two types of situations would normally require different approaches, as discussed in Section 13.6, and hence, we need to see beyond expected values when addressing risk and identifying critical systems.

Apostolakis and Lemon (2005) argue that ideally the expected disutility approach $Eu(C)$ should be implemented. However, in the absence of a rigorous way of establishing the probabilities, they see themselves forced to resort to a simpler approach. We would add the problem of specifying the utility function (refer discussion in Section 13.6). There will be a strong degree of arbitrariness in the choice of the function u, and some decision-makers would also be reluctant to specify the utility function as it reduces their flexibility to weigh different concerns in specific cases. It is however outside the scope of this book to discuss the pros and cons of the expected utility approach and related theories such as Prospect theory (Kahneman and Tversky 1979) in detail. We refer the reader to an extensive literature on this topic, for example, Bedford and Cooke (2001), Watson and Buede (1987), Clemen (1996) and Aven (2012d).

Hence, there is no obvious best candidate to use as a criticality measure in this case.

Example 2: identifying critical infrastructure

The task is to identify critical infrastructure on a national level. The aim is to be able to better prioritise activities and resources. The identified critical infrastructure is to provide a basis for determining adequate protection and mitigation measures and hence reduce the vulnerabilities and risks. If an infrastructure is classified as critical, more resources will be used for this purpose than if the infrastructure is not defined as critical.

Suppose that we have agreed upon the values of concern (water supply, electric power, etc.). Let us refer to these as attributes $C_1, C_2, \ldots$ and the infrastructure as $IS_1, IS_2, \ldots$. Now, if an infrastructure IS has failed (or is impaired), the conditional expected consequences are $E[C_1|IS$ has failed], $E[C_2|IS$ has failed], ..., which we refer to as $E[C|IS$ has failed]. Obviously, we may have different failure modes for each infrastructure, and this leads to $E[C(i)|IS$ has failed], where i refers to the ith failure mode. A common procedure for identifying critical infrastructure is to base the evaluation on the $E[C(i)|IS$ has failed]'s.

However, this approach is subject to the same type of problems as we identified in the previous example:

Which failure modes and scenarios should form the basis for the analysis? If few failure modes and scenarios are defined, the consequences need to be based on expected values, given failure, which could produce poor predictions of the actual outcomes. Severe consequences may then be hidden in the expected values. And if many failure modes and scenarios are defined, extreme outcomes may be revealed, but their likelihood could be very small.

This leads again to a risk-informed approach, also taking into account the probabilities of the initiating events, which, in this case, is the probability of an infrastructure failure, either caused by an accident or by an intentional act. We can then define risk indices as in the previous example based on the expected loss and expected disutility. The expected loss may relate to the different concerns separately or it can be an integrated measure based on a transformation of all concerns to a common scale, as is often done in a risk matrix; see Table 11.1.

One may argue that uncertainties and the likelihood related to the initiating events should not be taken into account as any vulnerability will eventually be exposed. However, we quickly see that such a reasoning fails. We simply cannot design for or implement measures that can withstand all possible hazards and threats. In a practical world, we are faced with resource limitations. Hence, we need some way of identifying what is important and what is not so important, and in our view this cannot be done in a rational manner without also considering uncertainties and the likelihood related to the initiating events, that is, without considering risk. In a particular case, we may judge a vulnerability to be exposed with a probability close to 100%, but this would be based on a risk analysis. Obviously, we will not judge all events, hazards and threats, to be that likely.

There are large uncertainties related to when and how attackers will carry out an attack on a specific infrastructure. Historical data are not available as a basis for determining relevant probabilities. The use of expert judgements for assigning probabilities can be used, but they would not in general be considered established in a sufficiently rigorous way, as argued by Apostolakis and Lemon (2005). The probabilities can produce poor predictions.

We search for a way of classifying the infrastructure according to criticality and acknowledge that risk has to be taken into account. Following the recommendations of this book, we may choose to highlight expected values and uncertainties; see e.g. Section 12.2. Refer also to Aven (2009a). It is an essential point that risk is more than calculated probabilities and expected values.

13.10 On the difference between risk as seen from the perspectives of the analysts and management

Let us return to Chapter 2 and the definition and understanding of the risk concept. For the risk analysts, we may consider risk expressed by (C, Q) (and related metrics) and is conditional on K, the background knowledge of the analysts (which includes the assumptions made). We can write

Analyst risk description: $(C, Q|K)$.

But can risk seen from the decision-makers' perspective be conditional on K? Should it not be unconditional, as deviations from assumptions made also represent risk that could be important for the decision to be made? Yes, for the decision-makers, $(C, Q|K)$ needs to be replaced by the unconditional triplet (C, Q, K), in line with the description of risk used in Chapter 2. However, Q and K have to be adequately interpreted, also to include a judgment of the knowledge K. In the following, we provide some reflections and guidelines for how to define and perform these judgements, based on the discussion in Aven (2015).

For a decision-maker and manager, it is essential to think first risk, and not immediately the risk description produced by the analysts. Risk is (C, U), where C is the future consequences of the activity, and U is uncertainty: not knowing what the consequences C will be. They have to acknowledge that the analysts have made a choice of which metrics to look at and what measure Q to be used to describe the uncertainties and that these metrics and the measure Q are based on some background knowledge K that may, to a varying degree, be strong or weak.

Relevant questions to ask for the decision-maker and manager would be:

(a) How would the analyst team judge their own strength of knowledge?

(b) How would other experts (or more generally stakeholders) judge the strength of the knowledge K?

(c) How would they themselves judge the strength of the knowledge K, also taking into account the judgements made in (a) and (b)?

Based on these questions, we can formulate the following extended risk descriptions from the perspective of the decision-maker and manager:

(a) Risk description for decision-maker and manager: (C, Q, K, K_S), where K_S is the analyst team's own judgement of the strength of their knowledge K.

(b) Risk description for decision-maker and manager: (C, Q, K, K_{S_1}), where K_{S_1} is the other experts' (stakeholders') judgement of the strength of the knowledge K.

(c) Risk description for decision-maker and manager: $(C, Q, K, K_S, K_{S_1}, K_D)$, where K_D is the decision-maker's (manager's) judgement of the strength of the knowledge K, reflecting also K_S and K_{S_1}.

In theory, we may have more than one group of other experts, but, to simplify, we allow for a maximum of one. The challenge is now to develop suitable ways of conducting the strength of knowledge judgements, K_S, K_{S_1} and K_D. The approach described in Section 2.4 represents one possible way to perform such strength of knowledge judgements. A similar approach can be formulated on the basis of the so-called NUSAP system, first proposed by Funtowicz and Ravetz (1990, 1993), see Aven (2015).

The decision-maker is not in general an expert on risk analysis and will simply have to acknowledge the risk characterisations of the risk analysts, with or without the input from other experts. He/she is not able to scrutinise the technical approach and methods used. Nonetheless, the decision-maker needs to make his/her own judgment about a number of issues, such as

- The input K_S and K_{S_1}

- Own assessment K_D of the strength of the knowledge K

- The implications of the analysts' and experts' results taking into account the limitations of the analyses, for example that the analysts lack important knowledge about the system studied. An issue here is also the risk related to deviations to key assumptions made.

- The implications of the analysts' and experts' judgements of the strength of the knowledge K, for example, the weight to be placed on the uncertainty characterisations Q when the background knowledge is considered rather weak.

- General quality considerations of the assessments. Key concepts in this respect are the reliability and validity terms. While reliability is concerned with the consistency of the "measuring instrument" (analysts, experts, methods, procedures), validity is concerned with the success at "measuring" what one sets out to "measure" in the analysis, see Aven and Heide (2009) and Aven (2011a). A topic here is the quality of the analysis team, for example, their experience and competence concerning the system studied and as risk analysts.

- Input from relevant concern assessments. Concern assessment is a term taken from the risk governance framework of Renn (2005). It can be viewed as a systematic process to comprehend the nature of effects and changes to the socio-economic environment and to express and evaluate these effects/changes and associated uncertainties.

- Other concerns (e.g. strategic issues if not covered by the above input.)

These are issues that the decision-maker takes into account in the decision-maker's review and judgement.

The decision-maker needs to be aware of the limitations of the risk analysis, for example, important uncertainty factors may be hidden in the background knowledge and the risk and uncertainty assessments may not be complete – hazardous situations could be overlooked. The analysts' and other experts' judgements of the strength of knowledge can be understood as an assessment of the related risk seen from the analysts' (and other persons') perspective. It provides an input to the decision-maker's and the manager's overall judgement. It is just an input, as it is limited by these groups' insights, competence and methods. The decision-maker (manager) has to question the degree to which all relevant input has been provided: could there have been data, information and knowledge available somewhere that should have been collected? And perhaps more work should be done to gain relevant data, information and knowledge (for example by testing and research).

Hence, the decision-maker (manager) needs to think about the overall quality of the analysis team, their experience and competence concerning the system studied and their role as risk analysts and experts. He/she needs to reflect on the status of the analysis work in general for the activity considered, for example, within the organisational unit. What are the competence and training standards? What is the culture like? Is there an excellence attitude? Are improvements highlighted and so on?

Assessing all these aspects represents a huge challenge for the decision-maker (manager). It is tempting to try to avoid such assessments and let the assessment prescribe what to do, going from a risk-informed situation to a risk-based one. In this way, if their actions turn out to be wrong (poor), they can claim absolution on the basis that "We did what the numbers told us to do. If the numbers were wrong, it's the analysts' fault" (Aven 2012c). There is, however, no way to escape from the responsibility for the decision-maker and manager – the use of a risk assessment to prescribe the decision making cannot be justified; there will always be aspects not reflected in the assessments; it is the decision-maker's and manager's job to make the decision, and they have to give the proper weight to the assessments. Then, they need to understand what these assessments are producing and what their constraints are.

It is not straightforward to use all this input in the decision-making process. Both quantitative and qualitative assessments form the basis. Many analysts and decision-makers consider the former input as more objective and valuable; the qualitative one is commonly referred to as subjective, lacking a scientific foundation. Such a view is, however, easily refuted. All risk descriptions are subjective, or at best inter-subjective among a set of analysts or experts. The point is that qualitative judgements are required to give an informative risk description as the quantitative one fails to capture all aspects, as argued for in Chapter 2. The choice one has to make is to stick to quantitative metrics based on $(C, Q|K)$ and ignore important risk features, or provide a broader and more complete risk description but then allow for qualitative judgements linked to K and its strength.

In some cases, when the issue concerns whether or not to accept a solution, conservative assumptions are often referred to as a useful tool to reduce the risk related to the background knowledge (Rosqvist and Tuominen 2004). If the decision criteria are met with conservative assumptions, one should be confident that the system is in fact a safe system. There could, of course, be cases where such an approach could be useful, but care has to be shown in not using best judgements in all parts of the assessment, as the results are then not easily interpreted. One may adopt some conservative assumptions, but how conservative should they be and which quantities should be covered? There are typically a large number of possibilities, and one can easily be misled to think that the system is safe because some conservative assumptions have been made but fail to reflect uncertainties and lack of knowledge linked to other quantities. It is better in general, therefore, to strive for balanced risk descriptions and let the policies for treating the risk take into account the uncertainties. Cautionary policies are often implemented to deal with risk and uncertainties, and being explicit about why such policies are implemented is more easily justified when the risk description seeks to provide fair characterisations of the uncertainties.

Regardless of the approach used to assess the strength of the knowledge, it is important to acknowledge that the assessments just constitute input to broader overall judgements that the decision-maker and manager need to conduct before a decision is made. The risk assessments, with their strength of knowledge considerations, are informing the decision-maker, not prescribing what to do, as frequently highlighted in this book. There is in general no formula that provides optimal decisions on the basis of risk assessments alone. Qualitative judgements are always required.

13.11 Conclusions

The traditional quantitative risk analyses provide a rather narrow risk picture, through calculated probabilities and expected values. We conclude that this approach should be used with care, in particular, for problems with large uncertainties. Alternative approaches highlighting the qualitative aspects are more appropriate in such cases. A "broad" risk description is required. This is also the case when there are different views related to the values to be protected and the priorities to be made. The main concern is the value judgements, but they should be supported by solid scientific analyses, also showing a broad risk picture. If one tries to demonstrate that it is rational to accept risk, on a scientific basis, a too narrow approach to risk has been adopted. Recognising uncertainty as a main component of risk is essential to "successfully" implement risk management.

What is a critical system or activity obviously depends on what we mean by critical. We need to specify whether we are concerned about risk or vulnerability and then refer to a risk critical system or a vulnerability critical system. If we are to establish a criticality ranking procedure of failed units as a basis for determining which units should be given priorities in the repair queue, we can establish a list of vulnerability critical units (e.g. by highlighting expected values and uncertainties given the occurrences of the initiating events). In most cases, however, risk is the key concept and expressions of risk should be used for the criticality ranking as discussed above.

A

Probability calculus and statistics

A.1   The meaning of a probability

A probability can be interpreted in different ways. In this book, we understand a probability to be an expression of how likely (credible) it is that an event will occur. Let us look at an example. Let A represent the event that a patient develops an illness, S, over the next year, when the patient shows symptoms, V. We do not know if A will occur or not – there is uncertainty associated with the outcome. However, we can have an opinion on how likely it is that the patient will develop the illness. Statistics show that about 5 out of 100 patients develop this illness over the course of 1 year if they show the symptoms V. Is it then reasonable to say that the probability that A will occur is equal to 5%? Yes, if this is all the information that we have available, then it is reasonable to say that the probability that the patient will become ill next year is 0.05 if the symptoms V are present. If we have other relevant information about the patient, our probability can be entirely different. Imagine, for example, that the particular patient also has illness B and that his/her general condition is slightly weakened. Then, it would be far more likely that the patient will develop illness S. The physician who analyses the patient may, perhaps, assign a probability of 75% for this case: For four such cases that are relatively similar, he/she predicts that three of four cases will develop the illness.

To make this a bit more formalised, we let $P(A|K)$ represent our probability that event A will occur, based on the background knowledge K. Often, we simplify the formula and write only $P(A)$. It is then implicit that the probability is based on the background knowledge K. If we say that the probability is 75%, then we mean that it is just as likely for event A to occur as it is to draw a red ball out of an urn that contains

Risk Analysis, Second Edition. Terje Aven.
© 2015 John Wiley & Sons, Ltd. Published 2015 by John Wiley & Sons, Ltd.

three red balls and one white ball. The uncertainty is the same. We see that we can understand probability also as being an expression of the uncertainty about what the outcome will be. It is, however, easier to think of probability as an expression of how likely (credible) it is that the event will occur.

Based on this line of thought, a correct or true probability does not exist. Even if one throws a dice, there is no correct probability. This may seem strange, but one must differentiate between proportions, observed or imaginary, and probability in the meaning in which we use the term here. Imagine throwing a dice a great many times – say, 6000 times. We would then obtain (if the dice is "normal") about 1000 showing a "1", about 1000 showing a "2" and so on. In the population of 6000 throws, the distribution will be rather similar to 1/6 for the various numbers. But imagine that we did an infinite number of trials. Then, the theory says that we would obtain exactly 1/6. However, these are proportions observed and resulting from imaginary experiments. They are not probabilities in our way of thinking. A probability applies to a defined event that we do not know will occur or not, and which is normally associated with the future. We will throw a dice. The dice can show a "4", or it can show a different number. Prior to throwing the dice, one can express one's belief that the dice will show a "4". As a rule, this probability is set to 1/6, because it will yield the best prediction of the number of "fours" if we make many throws. Using a "normal" (fair) dice, we will calculate that "four" will be the outcome in about 1/6 of cases in the long run.

However, there is nothing automatic in our assignment of the probability 1/6. We have to make a choice. We are the ones who must express how likely it is to obtain a "four", given our background knowledge. If we know that the dice is fair, then 1/6 is the natural choice. However, it is possible that one is convinced that the dice is not fair and that it will give many more "fours" than usual. Then, we may, for example, assign a probability $P(\text{'four'}) = 0.2$. No one can say that this is wrong, even though, one can check the proportion of "fours" for this dice in retrospect and verify its "normality". When one originally assigned the probability, the background knowledge was different. Probability must always be seen in relation to the background knowledge.

Classical statistics builds on an entirely different understanding of what probability is. Here, a probability is defined as a limit of a relative frequency, meaning the proportion given above when the number of trials becomes infinitely large. In this manner, "true" probabilities are established. These are then estimated using experiments and analyses. The reader is referred to Aven (2012d) for a discussion of this approach and the problems associated with it (see also Section 13.8).

A.2   Probability calculus

The rules of probability are widely known. We will not repeat them all here but will only briefly summarise some of the most important ones. The reader is referred to textbooks on probability theory.

Probabilities are numbers between 0 and 1. If the event A cannot occur, then $P(A) = 0$, and if A will occur for certain, then $P(A) = 1$. If the probability of an event is p, the probability that this event does not occur is $1 - p$. If we have two events, A and B, then the following formula holds:

$$P(A \text{ or } B) = P(A) + P(B) - P(A \text{ and } B)$$

$$P(A \text{ and } B) = P(A)P(B|A). \tag{A.1}$$

Here, $P(B|A)$ represents our probability for B when it is known that A has occurred. If A and B are independent, then $P(B|A) = P(B)$; in other words, the fact that we know that A has occurred does not affect our probability that B will occur.

Suppose that we want to express the probability that two persons will both develop illness S, if they both have symptoms V. In other words, we would like to determine $P(A_1 \text{ and } A_2|K)$, where A_1 represents patient 1 becoming ill and A_2 represents patient 2 becoming ill. We base our analysis on the assignments $P(A_1|K) = P(A_2|K) = 0.05$. Is then

$$P(A_1 \text{ and } A_2|K) = P(A_1|K) \cdot P(A_2|K) = 0.05^2 = 0.25\%?$$

The answer is "yes" if A_1 and A_2 are independent. But are they independent? If it was known to you that patient 1 had become ill, would it not alter your probability that patient 2 would become ill? Not necessarily – it depends on what your background knowledge is:

- what is known to us initially,

- whether there is a "coupling" between these patients in some way or another. For example, if they are both in a weakened physical condition or are related, then it is clear that we know more about patient 2 if we find out that patient 1 has become ill.

If our background knowledge is very limited, knowledge that patient 1 has become ill will provide information to us about patient 2. In practice, however, we have so much knowledge about this illness that we can ignore the information that is associated with A_1. We therefore obtain independence since

$$P(A_2|K, A_1) = P(A_2|K).$$

If there is coupling between the patients, as illustrated above, then $P(A_2|K, A_1)$ will be different from $P(A_2|K)$. Thus, we have a dependence between the events A_1 and A_2.

A conditional probability, $P(A|B)$, is defined by the formula

$$P(A|B) = P(A \text{ and } B)/P(B).$$

We see that this formula is simply a rewriting of formula (A.1). By substituting $P(A \text{ and } B)$ with $P(A)P(B|A)$ (again we use formula (A.1)), the well-known Bayes' formula is established:

$$P(A|B) = P(A)P(B|A)/P(B).$$

We will show the application of this formula in Section A.5.

A.3   Probability distributions: expected value

Let X denote the number of persons who become ill in the course of 1 year for a group of four persons. Assume that you have established the following probabilities that X will take the value i, $i = 0, 1, 2, 3, 4$:

i	0	1	2	3	4
$P(X = i)$	0.05	0.40	0.40	0.10	0.05

The expectation, EX, is defined by:

$$EX = 0 \cdot 0.05 + 1 \cdot 0.40 + 2 \cdot 0.40 + 3 \cdot 0.10 + 0.05 \cdot 4 = 1.7$$

The expected value is the centre of gravity of the distribution of X. If a lever is set up over the point 1.7, then the masses $0.05, 0.40, \ldots, 0.05$ over the points $0, 1, \ldots, 4$ will be perfectly balanced.

If X can assume one of the values $x_1, x_2, \ldots$, one can find EX by multiplying x_1 with the corresponding probability P_1, and likewise multiply value x_2, with probability P_2 and so on, and sum up all values x_j, that is,

$$EX = x_1 \cdot P_1 + x_2 \cdot P_2 + \ldots$$

If X denotes the number of events of a certain type, and this number is either 0 or 1, then the associated probability equals the expected value. This is evident from the formula for expected value, as in this case EX is equal to $1 \cdot P$ (the event will occur). In many situations, we are concerned about rare events in which we, for all practical purposes, can disregard the possibility of two or more such events occurring during the time interval under consideration. The expected number of events will then be approximately equal to the probability that the event will occur once.

In applications, we often use the term "frequency" for the expected value with respect to the number of events. We speak about the frequency of gas leakages, for example, when we actually mean the expected value. We can also regard the frequency as an observation, or prediction, of the number of events during the course of a certain period of time. If we say, for example, that the frequency is 2 per year, we have observed, or we predict, two events per year on average.

The expectation constitutes the centre of gravity of the distribution, as mentioned above, and we see from the example distribution that the actual outcome can be far from the expected value. To describe the uncertainties, a prediction interval is often used. A 90% prediction interval for X is an interval $[a, b]$, where a and b are constants, which is such that $P(a \leq X \leq b) = 0.90$. In cases where the probabilities cannot be determined such that the interval has a probability of 0.90, the interval boundaries are specified such that the probability is larger than, and as close as possible to, 0.90. In our example, we see that $[1, 3]$ is a 90% prediction interval. We are 90% certain that X will assume one of the values 1, 2 or 3.

The variance and standard deviation are used to express the spread around the expected value. The variance of X, $\text{Var}X$, is defined as the expectation of $(X - EX)^2$, while the standard deviation is defined as the square root of the variance.

A.3.1   Binomial distribution

Let us assume that we have a large population, I, of people (e.g. patients) and that we are studying the proportion q of them that become ill over the course of the next year. Let us assume further that we have another similar population II that is composed of n persons. Let X represent the number that develops the illness in this population. What is then our probability that all of those in population II will develop the illness, that is, $P(X = n)$?

Alternatively, we may think of the population comprising technical units, for example, machines. In the Bayesian literature, it is common to refer to q as a *chance* (Singpurwalla 2006).

To answer this question, first assume that q is known. You know that the proportion within the larger population I is 0.10, say. Then, the problem boils down to determining $P(X = n|q)$. If we do not have any other information, it would be natural to say that

$$P(X = n|q) = q^n.$$

We have n independent trials and our probability for "success" (illness) is q in each of these trials. We see that when q is known, then X has a so-called binomial probability distribution, that is,

$$P(X = i|q) = \frac{n!}{i!(n - i)!}q^i(1 - q)^{n-i}, i = 0, 1, 2, \ldots, n, \tag{A.2}$$

where $i! = 1 \cdot 2 \cdot 3 \cdot \ldots \cdot i$. The reader is referred to a textbook on probability calculus if understanding this is difficult.

When q is small and n is large, we can approximate the binomial probability distribution by using the Poisson distribution:

$$P(X = i|r) = \frac{r^i e^{-r}}{i!}, i = 0, 1, 2, \ldots,$$

where $r = nq$. We know, for example, that $(1 - q)^n$ is approximately equal to e^{-r}. This can be checked using a pocket calculator.

We refer to q and r as parameters of the probability distributions. By varying the parameters, we obtain a class of distributions.

What do we do if q is unknown? Let us imagine that q can be 0.1, 0.2, 0.3, 0.4 or 0.5. We then use the total probability rule and obtain:

$$P(X = i) = P(X = i|q = 0.1)P(q = 0.1) + P(X = i|q = 0.2)P(q = 0.2) + \ldots$$
$$+ P(X = i|q = 0.5)P(q = 0.5).$$

By assigning values for $P(q = 0.1), P(q = 0.2)$ and so on, we obtain the probability distribution for X, that is, $P(X = i)$ for various values of i.

A.4   Statistics (Bayesian statistics)

In statistics, focus is often on properties within large populations, for example, q in the above example, that is, the proportion of the large population I that will develop the illness in question. The problem is how to express our knowledge of q based on the available data X, that is, to establish a probability distribution for q when we observe X. We call this distribution the *posterior probability distribution* of q.

We begin with the so-called prior distribution before we perform the measurements X. Here let us suppose that we only allow q to assume one of the following five values: 0.1, 0.2, 0.3, 0.4 or 0.5. We understand these values such that, for example 0.5, this means that q lies in the interval $[0.45, 0.55)$.

Based on the available knowledge, we assign a prior probability distribution for the proportion q:

q'	0.1	0.2	0.3	0.4	0.5
$P(q = q')$	0.05	0.20	0.50	0.20	0.05

This means that we have the greatest confidence that the proportion q is 0.3 (50%), then 0.2 and 0.4 (20% each) and least likely, 0.1 and 0.5 (5% each).

Suppose now that we observe 10 persons and that among these persons there is only 1 that has the illness. How will we then express our uncertainty regarding q?

We use Bayes' formula and establish the posterior distribution of q. Bayes' formula states that $P(A|B) = P(B|A)P(A)/P(B)$ for the events A and B. If we apply this formula, we see that the probability that the proportion will be equal to q' when we have observed that 1 out of 10 has the illness is given by

$$P(q = q'|X = 1) = cf(1|q')P(q = q'), \tag{A.3}$$

where c is a constant such that the sum over the $q's$ is equal to 1, and f is given by

$$f(i|q') = P(X = i|q = q'),$$

refer formula (A.2); the quantity X is binomially distributed with parameters 10 and q' when $q = q'$ is given.

Using the formula (A.3), we find the following posterior distribution for q:

q'	0.1	0.2	0.3	0.4	0.5
$P(q = q')$	0.14	0.38	0.43	0.05	0.004

We see that the probability mass has shifted to the left towards smaller values. This was as expected since we observed that only 1 out of 10 became ill, while we, at the start, expected the proportion q to be closer to 30%.

If we had a larger observation set, then this data set would have dominated the distribution to an even larger degree.

B

Introduction to reliability analysis

In a risk analysis, we are concerned about the reliability of various systems, especially barrier and safety systems, and also equipment associated with production, for example, pumps and compressors in a processing plant. By reliability, we mean the ability of the system to function as planned. We express this ability using probabilities and expected values. A separate discipline, reliability analysis, has evolved for studying the reliability of such systems. In this appendix, we briefly summarise some important principles and methods used within this discipline. The reader is referred to Aven and Jensen (1999, 2013) for a more detailed coverage and relevant literature.

B.1   Reliability of systems composed of components

A system, for example, a gas detection system, is composed of n components (detectors) connected in parallel, that is, the system functions so long as one of the components functions; see Figure B.1. The existence of a connection between a and b means that the system functions. Let p_i represent the probability that component i functions at a certain point in time, $i = 1, 2, \cdots, n$, and let $q_i = 1 - p_i$. We refer to p_i and q_i as the reliability and the unreliability, respectively, of component i. The problem is now to compute the reliability (unreliability) of the system, that is, the probability that the system functions (does not function). For the sake of simplicity, we consider two components only, that is, $n = 2$.

Let $X_i = 1$ if component i functions and 0 otherwise. The unreliability of the system is then

$$P(\text{the system does not function}) = P(X_1 = 0 \text{ and } X_2 = 0).$$

Risk Analysis, Second Edition. Terje Aven.
© 2015 John Wiley & Sons, Ltd. Published 2015 by John Wiley & Sons, Ltd.

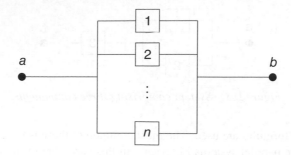

Figure B.1   Parallel system.

Figure B.2   Series system.

It follows that if the components are independent, then

$$P(\text{the system does not function}) = P(X_1 = 0)P(X_2 = 0) = q_1 q_2,$$

and thus $P(\text{the system functions}) = 1 - q_1 q_2$. If we do not have independence, the following formula applies:

$$P(\text{the system does not work}) = P(X_1 = 0)P(X_2 = 0 | X_1 = 0);$$

refer Appendix A.2.

With three or more components connected in parallel, the calculations are analogous. For a series system, we proceed in the same manner as for the parallel system, with a focus on the system functioning as opposed to not functioning. A series system functions if all of its components function; see Figure B.2. It follows that the reliability of the system is equal to the product of the reliability of the component reliabilities, again under the assumption of independence.

If the system is more complex, the calculation also becomes more complex. Consider, for example, a system that is composed of three components, where components 1 and 2 are connected to each other in parallel, and in series with component 3; see Figure B.3.

We then obtain the system reliability by multiplying the reliability of the parallel system and that of component 3, that is,

$$P(\text{the system functions}) = (1 - q_1 q_2)p_3.$$

This method can be used for larger systems as well, but becomes too time-consuming if the number of components reaches as high as, for example, 50. In such cases,

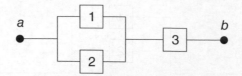

Figure B.3   System comprising three components.

approximation formulas are used. The most common of these is to sum up the unreliabilities of the parallel systems in series – in this case, that of the parallel system comprising components 1 and 2, and the system comprising component 3. We then obtain

$$P(\text{the system does not function}) \approx q_1 q_2 + q_3.$$

We refer to Section 6.6, where this method is described in more detail.

How are p and q determined? We differentiate between two example cases: a production system and a safety system.

B.2   Production system

Let us first look at a component. This component functions for a certain period of time, and then it fails. It is repaired and then put back into operation again, and the process is repeated. Let MTTF (Mean Time To Failure) and MTTR (Mean Time To Repair) represent the expected time to failure and the expected duration of the repair of the component, respectively. It would then be reasonable to set the probability q that the component does not function (is in a failure mode, that is, under repair) equal to $MTTR/(MTTF + MTTR)$. For example, if the component has an $MTTF = 990$ hours and an $MTTR = 10$, the unreliability q will then be $10/1000 = 0.01 = 1\%$. When repair is involved, we often use the term "availability" instead of "reliability". We interpret this to mean that the component is down 1% of the time. Often MTTR is much less than MTTF, as in this numerical example, and we can substitute $MTTR/(MTTF + MTTR)$ with $MTTR/MTTF$. If we let $r = 1/MTTF$, we obtain the commonly used formula for the unavailability, $q = rMTTR$. The quantity r is called the *failure rate of the component*. Here $r = 1/990$, in other words, one failure on average every 1000 hours approximately.

In the case of several independent components, we can substitute the q values with $MTTR/(MTTF + MTTR)$ or $rMTTR$, and calculate the availability of the system.

B.3   Safety system

First look at a component, for example, a gas detector. We denote the lifetime of the detector by T. The probability distribution of T is denoted by $F(t)$, for values

$t \geq 0$. The distribution F is given by $F(t) = P(T \leq t)$. Examples of distributions that are often used are the exponential distribution and the Weibull distribution; see, for example, Aven and Jensen (1999, 2013). For a given time t, unreliability of the component is given by

$$q = F(t).$$

In cases with several independent components, we can substitute the probabilities q with $F(t)$ and calculate the system reliability.

Again, look at the case where we have only one component, and let us assume that the component is tested at regular time intervals L, for example, once per month. The state of the component, that is, whether the component is functioning or not, will be revealed by the test.

In such a case, unreliability for the component is given as $F(t)$ for $t < L$. Following a test, we can assume that the component is as good as new, so that the reliability at time t, $L \leq t < 2L$, is the same as for $t < L$. The same applies for the third interval and so on.

Again, we can easily proceed to the system level and calculate the reliability of the system.

Another reliability index that is used in this case is the mean fractional dead time, which expresses the proportion of time that the component (system) is not functioning. The reader is referred to textbooks on reliability analysis, for example, Aven and Jensen (1999, 2013).

C

Approach for selecting risk analysis methods

The reader is referred to Section 3.2.2. In this appendix, we present an approach for the selection of a risk analysis method based on three aspects: expected consequences, uncertainties and frame conditions. A scheme for ICT-related problems is used to illustrate the approach.

C.1 Expected consequences

We refer to Table C.1. The expected consequences are expressed as the product of the probability that an event will occur (in this case, a fault in the ICT system) and expected consequences should such an event occur. The top rows in the table give the expected consequences for the different consequence categories (attributes). The excepted consequences, given failure, are addressed on two levels, expected effect on society and expected effect on the business. The bottom rows show the probabilities for various types of failures. Both probability and expected value are classified in broad categories: low, moderate and high, suitably defined. The italicised text show the results from the analysis.

In order to sum up the results from Table C.1, we use a $3 \cdot 3$ risk matrix with the expected consequences (given the occurrence of an undesirable event) plotted on one axis and probability on the other. We refer to this matrix as risk matrix 1. In Figure C.1, the results from the example are presented. The transfer to the risk matrix is based on a set of rules defined as follows:

- If the expected consequences (given the undesirable event) are given the score "high" for one or more dimensions (personal safety, reputation, etc.), the system is entered into the matrix with high expected consequences.

Risk Analysis, Second Edition. Terje Aven.
© 2015 John Wiley & Sons, Ltd. Published 2015 by John Wiley & Sons, Ltd.

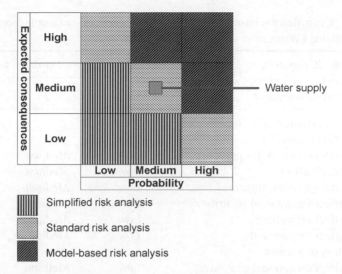

Figure C.1   Risk matrix 1 for water supply example. Expected consequences given the occurrence of a failure.

- If the probability of the undesirable event is given the score "high" for at least one factor, the system obtains a high probability score in the matrix.

Because different dimensions are being compared, Table C.1 involves an element of value judgement.

As shown in the example, the activity is classified as moderate in terms of expected consequences and moderate in terms of the probability that the undesirable event will occur. On the basis of this result, the procedure recommends the use of a standard risk analysis method. Subsequent evaluation criteria may, however, modify this.

C.2   Uncertainty factors

A scheme for assessing the factors that can produce significant deviation between the expected value and the actual consequence is shown in Table C.2. The questions refer to the complexity of the technology, organisation, available information and time frames for the assessment. Other factors can also be relevant, such as manageability and design vulnerabilities.

Risk matrix 2 in Figure C.2 summarises the results from Table C.2 for the example. The same principle used for risk matrix 1 (see Section C.1) is used in the transfer of the information from Table C.2 to the matrix Figure C.2. In the example, the score for uncertainty is "low"; in other words, we do not envisage any Surprise events with respect to the expected value analysis carried out above. We have a good understanding of the system and the problems involved. Hence, the recommendation is now a simplified risk analysis.

Table C.1   Classification based on expected consequences – example from a water supply operation (Wiencke et al. 2006).

Failure of the ICT system, (with respect to availability, confidentiality or integrity)	Score		
	1	*2*	*3*
Expected consequences of failure			
Expected effect on society			
Expected effect on safety for personnel	Low	*Medium*	High
Expected health effect	Low	*Medium*	High
Expected effect on environment	Low	*Medium*	High
Expected effect for national security	*Low*	Medium	High
Expected effect on welfare	Low	*Medium*	High
Expected effect on personal information protection	*Low*	Medium	High
Expected effect on national economy	*Low*	Medium	High
Expected effect on · · ·	*Low*	Medium	High
Expected effect on business			
Expected effect on business economy	*Low*	Medium	High
Expected effect on SHE performance	*Low*	Medium	High
Expected effect on business reputation	Low	*Medium*	High
Expected effect on business deliverables	Low	*Medium*	High
Expected effect on · · ·	Low	Medium	High
Probabilities of failure			
Probability of security problem attractiveness to external and internal groups of individuals	*Low*	Medium	High
Probability of failure due to extreme weather geographical distribution, technology, age, · · ·	*Low*	Medium	High
Probability of failure due to accidental events fire, flood, design philosophy, redundancy, · · ·	Low	*Medium*	High
Probability of failure due to human error, design philosophy, redundancy, · · ·	*Low*	Medium	High
Probability of failure due to technical breakdown	Low	*Medium*	High

Table C.2   Factors that can produce a significant deviation between the expected value and the actual consequences – an example from water supply operations.

Failure of the ICT system (either with respect to availability, confidentiality or integrity)	Score		
	1	2	3
Important factors (that could cause large deviations between the expected values and the actual consequences)			
Complexity of technology (unproven, interface with other systems and geographical distribution)	*Low*	Medium	High
Complexity of organisation (complex user organisation, many interface, ICT competences, safety culture, etc.)	*Low*	Medium	High
Availability of information (project phases: design, construction and operation)	*High*	Medium	Low
Time frame to evaluate the lifetime of a system	*Short*	Medium	Long

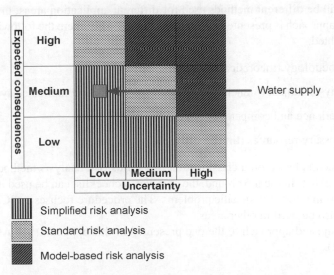

Figure C.2   Risk matrix 2 for water supply example.

A simple approach as the one presented here (Figure C.2 for instance) must be used with care. It may, for example, be problematic to use a model-based approach in some cases of high uncertainties, as the basis for developing the models could be weak. However, the risk analysis could lead to knowledge building and an improved platform for the construction of suitable models.

C.3   Frame conditions

Before making a final decision on whether a simplified, standard or model-based risk analysis method is to be used, the framework conditions such as time, budget and available information must be analysed. Table C.3 shows a scheme that can be used for analysing the framework conditions, using again the water supply example.

In the light of these analyses, it was concluded that a standard risk analysis method should be used.

C.4   Selection of a specific method

Both the checklist-based procedure presented in Section 3.2.1 and the risk-based one presented in Section 3.2.2 and expanded on in this appendix have the goal of indicating which category of method should be used: the simplified, standard or model-based method. The next step is to select a specific risk analysis method within this category.

There will be different methods used for different application areas. In Ford et al. (2007), an approach is presented for comparing methods, where the following aspects are highlighted:

1. Methodology (theoretical basis and approach)

2. Analysis subject (branches, individual subjects and complicated systems)

3. Experience and competency requirements

4. Necessary resources (time, money, etc.).

This approach is based on a classification of various risk analysis methods with the aid of a checklist. In the next round, the completed checklist can be used in selecting risk analysis methods for specific problems. The procedure focuses on ICT systems, but it can also be used in other areas.

For an adjusted approach to the one presented in this appendix, see Abrahamsen et al. (2012).

Table C.3 Frame conditions (example from a water supply operation).

Frame conditions	Analysis required and competences needed			Argument/comments
	Simplified risk analysis	Standard risk analysis	Model-based risk analysis	
Aim of the analysis	Action list	Overall risk picture, and prioritised action list	Overall risk picture, quantitative results and prioritised action list	Understand the threats/hazards exposing the system and the vulnerability of the system. Prioritising measures
Available resources for the risk and vulnerability analysis (budget and personnel)	Limited budget and competences on risk analysis	Competence in risk analysis is required, and good understanding of the system	Requires experience with model-based risk analysis and good understanding of the system	Good internal competence on the system. Limited recourses for external assistance if necessary
Schedule for the risk and vulnerability analysis	Limited time	Moderate time requirement	Require time for collecting data and establish models	To be completed this year
Experiences with similar systems (national or international)	Can use experiences from similar systems (checklists)	Has some experience	New system. Need to establish models to understand the system – events and consequences	Similar systems are used by a number of other water supply companies
Rules and regulations (requirements)				No requirement for specific methods

D

Terminology

This appendix summarises some risk analysis and management terminology used in the book. Reference is made to Aven (2011e), which discusses key terms based on the ISO standard on risk terminology (ISO 2009a,b).

1. **Aleatory uncertainty**
   Variation of quantities in a population

2. **Consequence**
   Outcome of an event
   When referring to the consequences of an activity, a broader definition is adopted, covering all types of events and outcomes associated with the activity.

3. **Event**
   Occurrence of a particular set of circumstances

4. **Frequentist probability**
   A frequentist probability $p(A)$ equals the fraction of times the event A occurs when the situation considered can be repeated over and over again under similar conditions
   A frequentist probability is a model concept, a parameter of a probability model.

5. **Interested party**
   Person or group having an interest in the performance of an organisation
   Examples are customers, owners, employees, suppliers, bankers, unions, partners or society.

Risk Analysis, Second Edition. Terje Aven.
© 2015 John Wiley & Sons, Ltd. Published 2015 by John Wiley & Sons, Ltd.

A group may be an organisation, part of an organisation or more than one organisation.

6. **Probability (subjective probability, knowledge-based probability or a judgmental probability)**
   A subjective measure of uncertainty of an event The probability is interpreted with reference to an uncertainty standard, for example, an urn: if the assessor assigns a probability of an event A equal to say 0.1, it means that the assessor compares his/her uncertainty (degree of belief) about the occurrence of the event *A* with drawing at random a specific ball from an urn that contains 10 balls.

7. **Risk**
   The two-dimensional combination of consequences (of the activity considered) and the associated uncertainties (what will be the consequences of the activity?)

8. **Risk acceptance**
   A decision to accept the risk

9. **Risk acceptance criterion**
   A reference by which risk is assessed to be acceptable or unacceptable

10. **Risk analysis**
    Systematic use of information and knowledge to identify sources, identify their causes and consequences and describe risk
    Risk analysis provides a basis for risk evaluation, risk treatment and risk acceptance. Information can include historical data, theoretical analysis, informed opinions and concerns of stakeholders.

11. **Risk assessment**
    Overall process of risk analysis and risk evaluation

12. **Risk criteria**
    Terms of reference against which the significance of the risk is assessed

13. **Risk evaluation**
    Process of comparing risk against given risk criteria to determine the significance of the risk
    Risk evaluation may be used to assist the decision-making process.

14. **Risk management**
    Coordinated activities to direct and control an organisation with regard to risk
    Risk management typically includes risk assessment, risk treatment, risk acceptance and risk communication.

15. **Risk treatment**
    Process to modify risk

16. **Source (risk source)**
    Element which alone or in combination has the intrinsic potential to give rise to a consequence
    The "consequence" focused is typically an undesirable outcome. A source in a safety context could be a hazard and in a security context a threat.

17. **Source identification**
    Process to find, list and characterise sources
    In the safety literature, source identification is called hazard identification.

18. **Stakeholder**
    Person or organisation that can be affected by, or perceive themselves to be affected by a decision or activity
    A decision-maker can be stakeholder. The term "stakeholder" includes but has a broader meaning than "interested party".

19. **Uncertainty about something**
    Not knowing this something, where "something" refers to the true value of a quantity or the true future consequences of an activity

20. **Uncertainty description**
    A measure of the uncertainty and associated background knowledge

21. **Vulnerability**
    The two-dimensional combination of the consequences (of the activity considered) and associated uncertainties (what will be the consequences of the activity?) given an initiating event (or a risk source).

D.1   Risk management: Relationships between key terms

- Risk assessment
  - Risk analysis
    - *Source identification*
    - *Cause analysis*
    - *Consequence analysis*
    - *Risk description*
  - Risk evaluation

- Risk treatment
  - Risk avoidance
  - Risk optimisation
  - Risk transfer
  - Risk retention
- Risk acceptance
- Risk communication

Bibliography

Abrahamsen, E.B., Aven, T., Pettersen, K.A., Rosqvist, T. (2012) A framework for selection of strategy for management of security measures. *Proceedings PSAM11 -ESREL2012*, Helsinki.

Anton, P.S., Anderson, R., Mesic, R. and Scheiern, M. (2003) The vulnerability assessment & mitigation methodology, Rand Report. ISBN 0-8330-3434-0.

Apostolakis, G.E. and Lemon, D.M. (2005) A screening methodology for the identification and ranking of infrastructure vulnerabilities due to terrorism. *Risk Analysis*, **24**(2), 361–376.

AS/NZS. (2004) 4360, Australian/New Zealand Standard: Risk Management.

Aven, T. (1992) *Reliability and Risk Analysis*. Elsevier, London.

Aven, T. (2007a) A unified framework for risk and vulnerability analysis and management covering both safety and security. *Reliability Engineering & System Safety*, **92**, 745–754.

Aven, T. (2007b) On the ethical justification for the use of risk acceptance criteria. *Risk Analysis*, **27**, 303–312.

Aven, T. (2008) A semi-quantitative approach to risk analysis, as an alternative to QRAs. *Reliability Engineering & System Safety*, **93**, 768–775.

Aven, T. (2009a) Identification of safety and security critical systems and activities. *Reliability Engineering & System Safety*, **94**, 404–411.

Aven, T. (2009b) Safety is the antonym of risk for some perspectives of risk. *Safety Science*, **47**, 925–930.

Aven (2010a) *Misconceptions of Risk*. John Wiley & Sons, Ltd, Chichester.

Aven, T. (2010b) On the need for restricting the probabilistic analysis in risk assessments to variability. *Risk Analysis*, **390**, 354–360. With discussion, **30**(3), 381–384.

Aven, T. (2010c) On how to define, understand and describe risk. *Reliability Engineering & System Safety*, **95**, 623–631.

Aven, T. (2010d) Some reflections on uncertainty analysis and management. *Reliability Engineering & System Safety*, **95**, 195–201.

Aven, T. (2011a) *Quantitative Risk Assessment: The Scientific Platform*. Cambridge University Press, Cambridge.

Risk Analysis, Second Edition. Terje Aven.
© 2015 John Wiley & Sons, Ltd. Published 2015 by John Wiley & Sons, Ltd.

Aven, T. (2011b) On the interpretations of alternative uncertainty representations in a reliability and risk analysis context. *Reliability Engineering & System Safety*, **3**, 353–360.

Aven, T. (2011c) A risk concept applicable for both probabilistic and non-probabilistic perspectives. *Safety Science*, **49**, 1080–1086.

Aven, T. (2011d) Selective critique of risk assessments with recommendations for improving methodology and practice. *Reliability Engineering & System Safety*, **96**, 509–514.

Aven, T. (2011e) On the new ISO guide on risk management terminology. *Reliability Engineering & System Safety*, **96**, 719–726.

Aven, T. (2011f) On different types of uncertainties in the context of the precautionary principle. *Risk Analysis*, **31**, 1515–1525.

Aven, T. (2012a) The risk concept - historical and recent development trends. *Reliability Engineering & System Safety*, **115**, 136–145.

Aven, T. (2012b) On when to base event trees and fault trees on probability models and frequentist probabilities in quantitative risk assessments. *International Journal of Performability Engineering*, **8**(3), 311–320.

Aven, T. (2012c) Foundational issues in risk assessment and management. *Risk Analysis*, **32**(10), 1647–1656.

Aven, T. (2012d) *Foundations of Risk Analysis*, 2nd ed. John Wiley & Sons, Inc., New York.

Aven, T. (2013a) A conceptual framework for linking risk and the elements of the data-information-knowledge-wisdom (DIKW) hierarchy. *Reliability Engineering & System Safety*, **111**, 30–36.

Aven, T. (2013b) How to define and interpret a probability in a risk and safety setting. Discussion paper, with general introduction by Associate Editor, Genserik Reniers. *Safety Science*, **51**, 223–231.

Aven, T. (2013c) On blacks swans in a risk context. *Safety Science*, **57**, 44–51.

Aven, T. (2013d) Practical implications of the new risk perspectives. *Reliability Engineering & System Safety*, **115**, 136–145.

Aven, T. (2014) *Risk, Surprises and Black Swans*. Routledge, New York.

Aven, T. (2015) *On the difference between risk as seen from the perspectives of the analysts and management*. Paper submitted for possible publication.

Aven, T. and Abrahamsen, E.B. (2007) On the use of cost-benefit analysis in ALARP processes. *International Journal of Performability Engineering*, **3**, 345–353.

Aven, T., Baraldi, P., Flage, R. and Zio, E. (2013) *Uncertainty in Risk Assessments*. John Wiley & Sons, Ltd, Chichester.

Aven, T., Hauge, S. Sklet, S. and Vinnem, J.E. (2006) Methodology for incorporating human and organizational factors in risk analyses for offshore installations. *International Journal of Materials and Structural Reliability*, **4**, 1–14.

Aven, T. and Heide, B. (2009) Reliability and validity of risk analysis. *Reliability Engineering & System Safety*, **94**, 1862–1868.

Aven, T. and Jensen, U. (1999, 2013) *Stochastic Models in Reliability*, 2nd ed. 2013. Springer-Verlag, New York.

Aven, T. and Kristensen, V. (2005) Perspectives on risk - review and discussion of the basis for establishing a unified and holistic approach. *Reliability Engineering & System Safety*, **90**, 1–14.

Aven, T. and Krohn, B.S. (2014) A new perspective on how to understand, assess and manage risk and the unforeseen. *Reliability Engineering & System Safety*, **121**, 1–10.

Aven, T., Nilsen, E. and Nilsen, T. (2004) Economic risk - review and presentation of a unifying approach. *Risk Analysis*, **24**, 989–1006.

Aven, T. and Pedersen, L.M. (2014) On how to understand and present the uncertainties in production assurance analyses, with a case study related to a subsea production system. *Reliability Engineering & System Safety*, **124**, 165–170.

Aven, T. and Renn, O. (2009a) On risk defined as an event where the outcome is uncertain. *Journal of Risk Research*, **12**, 1–11.

Aven, T. and Renn, O. (2009b) The role of quantitative risk assessments for characterizing risk and uncertainty and delineating appropriate risk management options, with special emphasis on terrorism risk. *Risk Analysis*, **29**, 587–600.

Aven, T., Renn, O. and Rosa, E. (2011) On the ontological status of the concept of risk. *Safety Science*, **49**, 1074–1079.

Aven, T., Røed, W. and Wiencke, H.S. (2008) *Risk Analysis*. The University Press, Oslo (in Norwegian).

Aven, T. and Vinnem, J.E. (2005) On the use of risk acceptance criteria in the offshore oil and gas industry. *Reliability Engineering & System Safety*, **90**, 15–24.

Aven, T. and Vinnem, J.E. (2007) *Risk Management, with Applications from the Offshore Oil and Gas Industry*. Springer-Verlag, New York.

Aven, T., Vinnem, J.E. and Wiencke, H.S. (2007) A decision framework for risk management. *Reliability Engineering & System Safety*, **92**, 433–448.

Aven, T. and Zio, E. (2011) Some considerations on the treatment of uncertainties in risk assessment for practical decision-making. *Reliability Engineering & System Safety*, **96**, 64–74.

Bedford, T. and Cooke, R. (2001) *Probabilistic Risk Analysis: Foundations and Methods*. Cambridge University Publishing Ltd., Cambridge.

van der Borst, M. and Schoonakker, H. (2001) An overview of PSA importance measures. *Reliability Engineering & System Safety*, **72**, 241–245.

Cabinet Office. (2002) *Risk: improving government's capability to handle risk and uncertainty*. Strategy Unit Report.

Campbell, S. (2005) Determining overall risk. *Journal of Risk Research*, **8**, 569–581.

Clemen, R.T. (1996) *Making Hard Decisions*, 2nd ed. Duxbury Press, New York.

Dondossola, G., Lamquet, O. and Masera, M. (2004) Emerging standards and methodological issues for the security analysis of power system information infrastructures. In *Proceedings of the Securing Critical Infrastructures*, Grenoble, October 2004.

Douglas, E.J. (1983) *Managerial Economics: Theory, Practice and Problems*, 2nd ed. Prentice Hall, Englewood Cliffs, NJ.

Duijm, N.J. and Goossens, L. (2006) Quantifying the influence of safety management on the reliability of safety barriers. *Journal of Hazardous Materials*, **130**(3), 284–292.

Falla, M. (1997) *Advances in Safety Critical Systems. Results and Achievements from the TI/EPSRC R&D Programme in Safety Critical Systems Compiled*. M. Falla (ed.): June 1997. http://www.comp.lancs.ac.uk/computing/resources/scs/. Accessed 14 April 2015.

Fischhoff, B., Lichtenstein, S., Slovic, P., Derby, S.L. and Keeney, R.L. (1981) *Acceptable Risk*. Cambridge University Press, Cambridge.

Flage, R., Amundrud, Ø. and Wiencke, H.S. (2014) Overall regional risk analysis of four Norwegian municipalities. *Proceedings ESREL 2014 Conference*, Wroclaw.

Flage, R. and Aven, T. (2009) Expressing and communicating uncertainty in relation to quantitative risk analysis (QRA). *Reliability and Risk Analysis: Theory and Applications*, **2**(13), 9–18.

Ford, E., Aven, T., Wiencke, W. and Røed, W. (2007) An approach for evaluating methods for risk and vulnerability assessments. *Proceedings of ESREL 2007*. Stavanger, June 25–27.

Funtowicz, S.O. and Ravetz, J.R. (1990) *Uncertainty and Quality in Science for Policy*. Kluwer Academic Publishers, Dordrecht.

Funtowicz, S.O. and Ravetz, J.R. (1993) Science for the post-normal age. *Futures*, **25**, 735–755.

Garrick, B.J., Hall, J.E., Kilger, M., McDonald, J.C., O'Toole, T., Probst, P.S., Parker, E.R., Rosenthal, R., Trivelpiece, A.W., Van Arsdale, L.A. and Zebroski, E.L. (2004) Confronting the risks of terrorism: making the right decisions. *Reliability Engineering & System Safety*, **86**, 129–176.

Gheorghe, A.V., Masera, M., Weijnen, M. and Vries, L.D. (2006) *Critical Infrastructures at Risk*. Springer-Verlag, Dordrecht.

Graham, J.D. and Weiner, J.B. (eds.) (1995) *Risk Versus Risk: Tradeoffs I Protecting Health and the Environment*. Harvard University Press, Cambridge.

Guikema, S.D. (2007) Modeling intelligent actors in reliability analysis: an overview of the state of the art, in: V.M. Bier and N. Azaiez (eds.) *Combining Reliability and Game Theory*, Springer Series on Reliability Engineering. In press.

Guikema, S. (2009) Game theory models of intelligent actors in reliability analysis: an overview of the state of the art, in: V.M. Bier and A.M. Naceur (eds.) *Game Theoretic Risk Analysis of Security Threats, International Series in Operations Research & Management Science*, vol. **128**. *Springer-Verlag, New York*.

Guikema, S. and Aven, T. (2010) Assessing risk from intelligent attacks: a perspective on approaches. *Reliability Engineering & System Safety*, **95**, 478–483.

Haimes, Y.Y. (2004) *Risk Modelling, Assessment, and Management*, 2nd ed. John Wiley & Sons, Ltd, New York.

Henley, E.J. and Kumamoto, H. (1981) *Reliability Engineering and Risk Assessment*. Prentice-Hall, New York.

Hjorteland, A., Aven, T. and Østebø, R. (2007) On how to treat uncertainty in regularity analyses, in different project phases. *Reliability Engineering & System Safety*, **92**, 1315–1320.

Hollnagel, E. (2004) *Barriers and Accident Prevention*. Ashgate Publishers, Aldershot.

HSE. (2001) *Reducing Risk, Protecting People*. HES Books, ISBN 0 71 762 151 0.

HSE. (2003) *Guidance on ALARP for Offshore Division Inspectors Making an ALARP Demonstration*. 1/10-03.

HSE. (2006) *Offshore Installations (Safety Case) Regulations*. HSE Books, London.

IEC. (2003) 61 511, Functional Safety: Safety Instrumented System for the Process Industry Sector, part 1–3, December 2003. ISO.

ISO. (2008) ISO/CD 20 815, Petroleum, Petrochemical and Natural Gas Industries - Production Assurance and Reliability Management. http://www.iso.org/iso/catalogue_detail.htm?csnumber=39744. Accessed 29 September 2014.

ISO. (2009a) Guide 73:2009, *Risk Management - Vocabulary*. ISO.

ISO. (2009b) 31000:2009, Risk Management - Principles and Guidelines. ISO.

Jenelius, E., Petersen, T. and Mattson, L.-G. (2006) Importance and exposure in road network vulnerability analysis. *Transportation Research Part A*, **40**, 537–560.

Jones-Lee, M.W. (1989) *The Economics of Safety and Physical Risk*. Basil Blackwell, Oxford.

Kahneman, D. and Tversky, A. (1979) Prospect theory: an analysis of decision under risk. *Econometrica*, **XLVII**, 263–291.

Kaplan, S. (1991) Risk assessment and risk management - basic concepts and terminology, in: *Risk Management: Expanding Horizons in Nuclear Power and Other Industries*. Hemisphere Publishing Corporation, Boston, MA, 11–28.

Kaplan, S. and Garrick, B.J. (1981) On the quantitative definition of risk. *Risk Analysis*, **1**, 11–27.

Knight, F.H. (1921) *Risk, Uncertainty and Profit*. Board Books, Washington, DC. Reprinted 2002.

Kristensen, V., Aven, T. and Ford, D. (2006) A new perspective on Renn & Klinke's approach to risk evaluation and risk management. *Reliability Engineering & System Safety*, **91**, 421–432.

Leva, M.C., Hansen, P.F., Sonne Ravn, E., Lepsøe, A. (2006) SAFEDOR: a practical approach to model the action of an officer of the watch in collision scenarios. *ESREL 2006*.

Leveson, N. (2004) A new accident model for engineering safer systems. *Safety Science*, **42**, 237–270.

Leveson, N. (2007) Modeling and analyzing risk in complex socio-technical systems. *NeTWork Workshop, Berlin, 27–29 September 2007*.

Levy, H. and Sarnat, M. (1990) *Capital Investment and Financial Decisions*, 4th ed. Prentice Hall, New York.

Lowrance, W. (1976) *Of Acceptable Risk - Science and the Determination of Safety*. William Kaufmann Inc., Los Altos, CA.

Lindley, D.V. (1985) *Making Decisions*. John Wiley & Sons, Ltd, London.

Löfstedt, R.E. (2003) The precautionary principle: risk, regulation and politics. *Transactions IChemE*, **81**, 36–43.

Modarres, M. (1993) *What Every Engineer Should Know About Risk*. Marcel Dekker, New York.

Mohaghegh, Z., Kazemi, R. and Mosleh, A. (2009) Incorporating organizational factors into Probabilistic Risk Assessment (PRA) of complex socio-technical systems: a hybrid technique formalization. *Reliability Engineering & System Safety*, **94** (2009), 1000–1018.

Norwegian Public Roads Administration. (2007) *Guidelines for Risk Analysis in Road Traffic Considerations*. Document in preparation.

Papazoglou, I.A., Bellamy, L.J., Hale, A.R., Aneziris, O.N., Ale, B.J.M., Post, J.G., Oh, J.I.H. (2003) I-Risk: development of an integrated technical and Management risk methodology for chemical installations. *Journal of Loss Prevention in the Process Industries*, **16**, 575–591.

Paté-Cornell, E.M. and Murphy, D.M. (1996) Human and management factors in probabilistic risk analysis: the SAM approach and observations from recent applications. *Reliability Engineering & System Safety*, **53**, 115–126.

PSA (2001) *Regulations Petroleum Safety Authority Norway*.

Rasmussen, J. (1997) Risk management in a dynamic society: a modelling problem. *Safety Science*, **27**(2/3), 183–213.

Rausand, M. and Høyland, A. (2004) *System Reliability Theory*, 2nd ed. John Wiley & Sons, Ltd, New York.

Renn, O. (1992) Concepts of risk: a classification, in: S. Krimsky and D. Golding (eds.) *Social Theories of Risk*. Praeger, Westport, pp. 53–79.

Renn, O. (2005) *Risk Governance: Towards an Integrative Approach*. White Paper No. 1, written by Ortwin Renn with an Annex by Peter Graham. International Risk Governance Council, Geneva.

Renn, O. (2008) *Risk Governance*. Earthscan, London.

Renn, O. and Klinke, A. (2002) A new approach to risk evaluation and management: risk-based precaution-based and discourse-based strategies. *Risk Analysis*, **22**, 1071–1094.

RESS. (2007) Reliab. Eng. Syst. Safe., 92(6), Special issue on critical infrastructures.

Rosa, E.A. (1998) Metatheoretical foundations for post-normal risk. *J. Risk Res.*, **1**, 15–44.

Rosa, E.A. (2003) The Logical Structure of the Social Amplification of Risk Framework (SARF); Metatheoretical Foundations and Policy Implications, in: N. Pidgeon, R.E. Kasperson and P. Slovic (eds.) *The Social Amplification of Risk*. Cambridge University Press, Cambridge, pp. 47–79.

Rosqvist, T. and Tuominen, R. (2004) Qualification of formal safety assessment: an exploratory study. *Safety Science*, **42**, 99–120.

Sandin, P. (1999) Dimensions of the precautionary principle. *Hum. Ecol. Risk Assess.*, **5**, 889–907.

Sandøy, M., Aven, T. and Ford, D. (2005) On integrating risk perspectives in project management. *Risk Manag.: Int. J.*, **7**, 7–21.

Singpurwalla, N. (2006) *Reliability and Risk. A Bayesian Perspective*. John Wiley & Sons, Ltd, New York.

Taleb, N.N. (2007) *The Black Swan: The Impact of the Highly Improbable*. Penguin, London.

Vatn, J. (2005) Assessment of the societal safety for the NOKAS cash depot. SINTEF report. 2005-04-12. (in Norwegian).

Vatn, J. (2007) Societal Security - a case study related to a cash depot. *Proceedings ESREL, 25–27 June 2007, Stavanger, Norway*.

Vinnem, J.E., Aven, T., Husebø, T., Seljelid, J., Tveit, O.J. (2006a) Major hazard risk indicators for monitoring of trends in the Norwegian offshore petroleum sector. *Reliability Engineering & System Safety*, **91**, 778–791.

Vinnem, J.E., Kristiansen, V. and Witsø, E. (2006b) Use of ALARP evaluations and risk acceptance criteria for risk informed decision-making in the Norwegian offshore petroleum industry. *Proceedings ESREL, 18–22, September 2006, Estoril, Portugal*.

Vose, D. (2008) *Risk Analysis, A Practical Guide*, 3rd ed. John Wiley & Sons, Ltd, New York.

Watson, S.R. and Buede, D.M. (1987) *Decision Synthesis*. Cambridge University Press, New York.

Wiencke, H.S., Aven, T. and Hagen, J. (2006) A framework for selection of methodology for risk and vulnerability assessments of infrastructures depending on ICT. *ESREL 2006*, pp. 2297–2304.

Wiencke, H.S., Tunes, T. and Kjestveit, K. (2007) Risk and vulnerability analysis for the Stavanger region. Report IRIS-2007/068 (in Norwegian).

Willis, H.H. (2007) Guiding resource allocations based on terrorism risk. *Risk Analysis*, **27**(3), 597–606.

Zio, E. (2013) *The Monte Carlo Simulation Method for System Reliability and Risk Analysis.*, Springer-Verlag, London.

Index

Risk Analysis, Second Edition. Terje Aven.
© 2015 John Wiley & Sons, Ltd. Published 2015 by John Wiley & Sons, Ltd.